Praise for
The Writer's Practice

"Warner generously offers useful hints for improving nonfiction writing. . . . Warner's style reads like informal, intelligent conversation founded on a genuine desire to share what he knows, and his helpful book will serve as a trusty companion to writers on their own or in class."
—*Publishers Weekly*

"In this uber-handy guide, veteran rhetorician Warner invites readers to sharpen their written communication skills. . . . The guide is well-organized and extremely readable, infused with the perfect amount of Warner's personality and experiences. Unique and thorough, Warner's handbook could turn any determined reader into a regular Malcolm Gladwell." —*Booklist*

"In *The Writer's Practice*, John Warner invites us on a quest. Quite literally—the book is no passive read, but instead an interactive journey. Warner lays out a map of writing challenges and puzzles (he calls them 'experiences'), provides tools for the odyssey, and keeps up a friendly, encouraging banter throughout. The experiences stretch one's writing practice in compelling ways, covering a wide variety of genres and skills. Completed collectively or selectively, the practices would assuredly benefit students, professionals, or anyone who desires to improve their writing."
—Sarah Rose Cavanagh, Assumption College, author of
*The Spark of Learning: Energizing the College Classroom with
the Science of Emotion*

"Think you can't write? John Warner disagrees. In his carefully plotted guide to better writing, Warner argues that with focused practice, you CAN improve. So can your students. *The Writer's Practice* offers an easy-to-follow series of lessons that, while prompting you to write,

build essential writing muscles. An ideal book for anyone new to teaching writing or for aspiring writers keen to improve their craft."
　　—Carol Jago, long-time high school English teacher, past president of the National Council of Teachers of English, and associate director of the California Reading and Literature Project, UCLA

"A fast and fun guide to what matters in writing (spoiler: attention to audience and purpose), covering everything from academic papers and business reports to travel guides, memoirs, jokes, and even obituaries. Warner writes for readers, and they'll love him for it—plus they'll learn to do the same."
　　—Daniel F. Chambliss, Eugene M. Tobin Distinguished Professor of Sociology, Hamilton College, and coauthor of *How College Works*

"With its focus on doing rather than explaining, *The Writer's Practice* invites collaboration. Whatever route readers takes through the book (and Warner outlines several possibilities), they will encounter new and challenging authorial tasks, helpfully contextualized. Working through the various sections, writers will practice the 'attitudes, skills, habit of mind, and knowledge' that Warner positions as critical to effective writing. The end product will be a sort of coauthored text, reflecting Warner's goals and methods, and the reader's effort and growth. Adaptable for classroom use but just as valuable for solo practitioners, *The Writer's Practice* is an indispensable guide for writers and instructors alike."
　　—Susan Schorn, Writing Program Coordinator, School of Undergraduate Studies, University of Texas–Austin

"John Warner's approach to nonfiction merges his experience as a creative writer and his expertise as a teacher of college composition. Rather than see creative and academic writing as opposed, Warner encourages the aspiring nonfiction writer to adopt a dual perspective: Analytical writing can be like a dialogue. A memory can be held up to the test of research. Too many writing tasks ask the student to regard their writing at a great distance, as if poking something vaguely distasteful or even dangerous. Warner's book encourages students to bring non-fiction writing closer to them, to embrace its complexity, its challenge, and its importance to their own lives."

—Catherine Prendergast, professor, dept. of English,
University of Illinois at Urbana–Champaign

"Practice? Writer's practice? Who's a writer?? You?? Me??? Claiming that everyone is a writer, experienced writer and writing teacher John Warner shares his insights about writing. It's not magic, but it takes practice—not a list of rules—to write well. He guides novices and even more seasoned writers to think about what they are trying to accomplish, and then how to make it happen. It's not the usual school-writing, thank goodness, so students and those guiding them will find it refreshing and even, possibly, enlightening. In his I'm-in-love-with-writing approach, Warner can't be stopped from sharing every trick he's stumbled upon. We all write. We can all write better. It's hard, and fun, and will change the way you look at communicating, and possibly the way you think about everything."

—Susan D. Blum, professor of anthropology, The University
of Notre Dame

"In *The Writer's Practice*, writer and writing teacher John Warner confesses: 'There's no one right way to write.' Throughout this how-to volume on nonfiction writing, Warner remains grounded in this paradox by avoiding templates while guiding writers as well as would-be writers and teachers through the questions and problems that all writers navigate in the pursuit of writing well. This book is a gift and everyone learning to write (thus, everyone), or seeking ways to teach writing better, must add this work to their essential bookshelf."

—P.L. Thomas, professor of education, Furman University,
and author of *Trumplandia: Unmasking Post-Truth America* and
*Teaching Writing as Journey, Not Destination: Essays Exploring
What "Teaching Writing" Means*

"While most writing textbooks devote a chapter to the rhetorical situation, John Warner's *The Writer's Practice* is the rare book whose activities center on the idea that good writing responds to the demands of its situation. Presenting a variety of authentic writing tasks, Warner's book shows students how to adapt their writing to address different audiences, even if that audience is oneself."

—Chris Warnick, College of Charleston

PENGUIN BOOKS

THE WRITER'S PRACTICE

John Warner has more than twenty years' experience teaching college-level writing, working with a range of students on developmental writing through graduate-level studies. He has taught many different types of writing, from composition, fiction, and narrative nonfiction to technical and humor writing. A contributing writer at *Inside Higher Ed*, he has become a national voice on writing pedagogy and writes a weekly column on books and reading for the *Chicago Tribune*. He is the author of five books. An editor-at-large at *McSweeney's*, he has worked with writers who have gone on to publish in outlets including *The New York Times*, *The New Yorker*, and *The Guardian*.

THE WRITER'S PRACTICE

*Building Confidence in
Your Nonfiction Writing*

JOHN WARNER

PENGUIN BOOKS

PENGUIN BOOKS

An imprint of Penguin Random House LLC
penguinrandomhouse.com

Library of Congress Cataloging-in-Publication
Control Number: 2018032895 (print)

ISBN 9780143133155 (paperback)
ISBN 9780525504931 (ebook)

Printed in the United States of America
11   13   15   17   19   20   18   16   14   12

Set in Dante MT with Archer
Designed by Sabrina Bowers

To my students:
past, present, and future

Contents

GETTING STARTED

Before We Begin . . .

Do me a favor and write down how to make a peanut-butter-and-jelly sandwich. You can even write it right in the book if you want. It's a good thing to write in books, and I've asked the publisher to leave some room.

WRITING EXPERIENCES

In this book, rather than "assignments" or "essays," I want us to consider what we're doing in terms of "experiences." While you've likely done lots of writing, for our purposes, you've just completed your first writing "experience." How did you do?

Take a moment to visualize what would happen if someone who is unfamiliar with making a peanut-butter-and-jelly sandwich could successfully make an acceptable sandwich with your instructions.

What would they do? What's missing?

For example, is there a line like "Take the peanut butter and spread it on one side of the bread"?

Picture someone following this instruction literally.

It does not tell this person how much peanut butter to spread or what to spread it with. A true literalist would actually be rubbing the closed peanut butter jar against a piece of bread.

Mmm . . . delicious.

Maybe this seems picky or ridiculous, but imagine leaving out key instructions for something not as mundane as making a peanut-butter-and-jelly sandwich.

Take a couple of minutes to see all the mistakes you might cause if someone followed your instructions to the letter.

LEARNING FROM EXPERIENCES

Do not feel bad if you now recognize your instructions as subpar. I set you up for failure. Over the years, I have asked hundreds, maybe thousands, of people, ranging from students to tenured professors to published writers, to prepare instructions for making a peanut-butter-and-jelly sandwich, and almost invariably they make very similar mistakes.

They make mistakes because I purposefully neglected to mention an audience in the instructions, and by not doing this I have induced them to be careless and inconsiderate of the audience's needs. This is forgivable since they didn't know the audience existed.

Most people, when asked to do this, write a vague description of themselves making a sandwich. In their minds, they picture the steps as *they* see them, rather than through the eyes of an inexperienced sandwich maker

Now that you are aware of an audience, you would likely change your directions in significant ways.

Being "audience aware" while working is one of the most important skills writers develop. Over time, it becomes second nature to ask yourself if the choices you're making are good ones.

You are already a more experienced writer with an improved appreciation for the role of the audience in writing, and we've just barely started.

Before we move on to more experiences, I want to answer some questions you might be having.

QUESTIONS ABOUT THIS BOOK

WHO IS IT FOR?

This book is for anyone who wants to improve their writing, which is everyone because everyone is a writer.

Think about it. You write all the time. You text, you e-mail, you interact on social media, you make lists, and you write for school or work or both. On any given day, you write thousands of words.

Writing is communication. If you're trying to convey a specific message to a specific audience to fulfill a specific purpose, you're writing

HOW DOES IT WORK?

We get better at writing the same way we get better at anything else: by doing it. This book is designed for doing things that allow you to practice the "writer's practice."

Yes, you are going to practice your practice: the attitudes, skills, habits of mind, and knowledge that writers engage with when they are writing. Ultimately, the goal is to think and act as a writer whenever you are confronted with a writing task.

You will practice your practice by engaging with different experiences, after which you will reflect on the experience to better understand what you've learned and can apply the next time you are confronted with a writing-related problem.

The experience of writing instructions for a peanut-butter-and-jelly sandwich has likely already allowed you to reflect on how important it is to consider your audience before you start writing. Now that we know that considering the audience is a key to effective communication, we will do it from this moment forward.

Writing is a skill, but it's a skill that can appear to disappear when we move from a familiar writing task to an unfamiliar writing task. Reflection is a way to transfer what we know about writing in one arena to a new arena by understanding the similarities and identifying the differences and adjusting accordingly.

It's like an athlete looking at game tape or a musician reviewing a performance. We're asking: What happened? What did I learn? What will I do differently the next time?

Eventually enough experience accrues and you have a battle-tested process for tackling any writing task, no matter how unfamiliar.

WHAT DO I NEED?

There are no prerequisites for having these experiences, and there is no one so experienced that they can't benefit from them. In fact, once I started thinking about writing as a series of experiences, I became a much better writer. When I need to write something unfamiliar, I now try to break it down as a writing experience. Once you've had enough experiences, you too will be able to take an unfamiliar writing task and break it down into its component parts.

You'll want to keep track of your writing experiences one way or another, but you should use the writing tools with which you're most comfortable. I'm a word-processing software person myself, but if you're a chisel and stone tablet type, all blessings to you.

In addition to the experiences themselves, I've included chapters designed to allow for deeper, big-picture reflection about what you're learning.

WILL THIS WORK IN A CLASS?

The experiences are designed to be adaptable to a class context. An instructor can add elements such as grading criteria, deadlines, word counts, specific readings, peer response, or anything else necessary to fit the structures and rhythms of school. Almost all of these experiences were born in the college classrooms in which I've worked for twenty years.

In the appendix, I've included possible assignment sequences that may be useful in planning a contained, semester-long course. It's important to remember that these are designed to be "experiences," and the meaning is in the doing. This leaves room for any necessary alterations to meet specific curricular needs or demands.

WHAT IF I'M WORKING ALONE?

Care has been taken to make all experiences self-contained and do-able on your own. Because we always write for audiences, at times you will be asked to find someone to test your writing's effectiveness on, but following the process will provide you with enough information and context to complete the experience and, in turn, increase your knowledge of and confidence in your own writing.

HOW DO I START?

You've already started. Now that you've started, you should try as many experiences as you like. Some can take as little as a few minutes, while others may stretch over days or weeks. Many of these experiences can be repeated over and over, and you will continue to learn new things each time.

Just like a musician, you may choose to "play" the same piece over and over, and find you become more deeply familiar with a particular writing experience each time around. The learning is always in the doing.

WHERE ARE WE GOING?

I have been writing seriously for more than twenty-five years and teaching for twenty. I am certain that everyone can learn to write, but to achieve this the writer must be in charge of their own learning.

This book is here to give shape to your practice, and encourage you to work purposefully toward increased proficiency.

While you will quite quickly amass experience, it's important to recognize that there is no terminal expertise in writing. You will get a little better every time you do it, but you will never reach a finish line after which you will cease to improve.

This is one of the best things about writing with purpose and writing through different experiences.

May as well keep going by next figuring out who you are as a writer.

Who Are You?

(As a Writer)

Earlier, I declared that you're already a writer. It's best to just embrace this identity right out of the gate. The definition of "writer" is someone who writes, so you qualify.

But what kind of writer are you?

When do you write? How do you write? What are your attitudes toward writing?

In this opening experience, you'll explore your previous experiences as a writer.

AUDIENCE

You're writing for someone who is curious to know about you and your experiences as a writer: what you've done, how you feel, what you hope to do.

They know nothing about you or your past experiences writing but want to get an idea of what you've done and where you're coming from.

PROCESS

1. Consider your past.

Before writing the piece itself, spend some time thinking about your experiences as a writer: what you've done, where you've done it, why you've done it.

Consider your attitudes toward these things you've done. How do you see yourself? What has shaped your views? Consider making a timeline that charts the kind of writing you've done at different times in your life.

2. Draft.

Remembering that your audience knows nothing about you, draft a communication to them that fulfills their needs. You'll write directly to your audience.

3. Revise.

Review your draft for coherence and structure. Are you telling the audience what they need to know and in an order that helps them understand your message? Are you exemplifying your message?

Think of it like a game of show-and-tell. Saying "I like writing" makes your experience vague and abstract to your audience. They're likely to wonder why you like writing or what sorts of things you like to write or when you like to write.

Instead, show your audience your message through examples that illustrate what you're telling them.

4. Edit and polish.

You're making your first impression on someone with whom you'll be working. Try to make the kind of impression you desire.

REFLECT

In the process of considering the audience as you were writing, hopefully you learned something about yourself.

Some questions to consider:

How diverse are your writing experiences? Have you written lots of different things or do you feel like you've mostly done variations of the same thing?

Which sounds more true to you: "I am a good/bad writer" or "I am good/bad at writing"? Why would you choose one over the other?

How much (if any) of your attitude about writing is linked to what happened in school and/or grades? What about other kinds of feedback you've received on your writing?

When have you most enjoyed writing? When have you least enjoyed it? What is the difference between those experiences?

You won't be surprised to hear me say that declaring you are good or bad, as though this is a fixed and immutable state, is not a great way to improve a skill. Even saying you are good or bad at writing probably isn't that helpful. Remember that there is no finish line for writers. Worry less about how good you are, and think more about how practicing writing will make you better.

REMIX

Considering your reflections, design your ideal writing situation. What kind of writing would you be doing? How would you be doing it? Who would be reading it? Who would be judging it? Where would you be writing? What would you be writing about?

Put this into a brief statement on its own, something that could fit on a four-by-six index card. Keep this nearby when you're writing as a way to reflect on what you're doing in the moment and to see if there are ways to bridge any gaps between the actual and the ideal by changing your point of view.

INTRODUCTION TO THE WRITER'S PRACTICE

The experiences in this book are designed to help you develop a writer's "practice."

But what do I mean by this? To start, think of a chef.

What makes a chef a chef?

A chef must have a chef's skills: knife work, cooking techniques, and the like. They also should have a deep knowledge of flavors and ingredients; how salt, fat, and acid combine to create different taste experiences; and how different cooking techniques bring out different qualities in the ingredients.

Chefs must be able to look in the refrigerator and pantry, and be able to assemble a meal. Chefs need to be able to plan and execute a dish, and juggle multiple tasks during the execution phase. They must be able to correct course when something looks off, and they need to have the confidence to know when something needs to go in the garbage rather than be served to diners, even if it means someone will grumble. All this makes up a chef's practice.

A practice consists of the practitioner's attitudes, skills, habits of mind, and knowledge. When I'm in the act of writing, I'm not consciously aware of these different aspects, because my "practice" has largely become second nature, but this is the goal: that when confronted with a writing-related task, your practice kicks in and starts solving the problem.

During any part of the writing process, a writer is engaging in the writer's practice. I'm doing it as I type these words, the same way a chef is when sautéing vegetables.

But I'm also doing it as I walk the dog, thinking about the projects I'm working on, just as a chef is when planning a menu. A teacher's practice isn't limited to the time in class but includes all the preparation that makes class possible. A practice is not something that begins and ends at the moment you're actively doing it. It is a method of continual processing and problem solving.

For the elements of a practice to become second nature, it helps to consider them deliberately.

Attitudes: what does a writer believe and value about the act of writing?

Skills: what can a writer do?

Habits of mind: how do writers think?

Knowledge: what does a writer know?

What do each of these look like as we're practicing our practice?

ATTITUDES

The first thing to know about writing is, in the words of Jeff O'Neal, a longtime writing teacher and now digital media entrepreneur, "You are going to spend your whole life learning how to write, and then you are going to die."

Even though this may seem daunting, it means writing will never get boring. As you work through the experiences in this book, you will absolutely gain a sense of your own growth and improvement, but you will never reach the finish line. There is no finish line. Perhaps I am perverse, but I find this sentiment comforting. Writing should never be boring, provided we are writing in ways that matter to us.

SKILLS

The experiences in this book are specifically and deliberately designed to provide opportunities to practice the skills associated with writing. In fact, the design is so deliberate that I often just come right out and say, "In this experience, we will be practicing . . ."

Big picture, a writer knows how to conceive, draft, revise, edit, and polish a piece of writing. However, almost innumerable skills underlie each part of the process,

- A writer, for example, knows how to target a message to achieve a specific purpose when communicating to a specific audience within a specific medium or genre. This is called analyzing the rhetorical situation. In other words, one writes to real people under different conditions, while trying to say something that meets their needs and conveys one's message.

- A writer must be able to do research appropriate to the rhetorical situation.

- A writer must be able to think "critically" in order to understand the impact of their own ideas on the audience, which includes understanding the ideas and emotions others will bring to the act of reading.

- A writer must be able to craft sentences that achieve their purposes in language appropriate for their occasion and audience.

Every experience in this book touches on these elements of the writer's practice, some more heavily than others, depending on the experience, but at a minimum you will always be writing to an audience to fulfill a specific purpose.

HABITS OF MIND

I have been writing for so long, I find I take writers' habits of mind for granted, so I must pause and think for a moment about what I think. What do I believe about writing? A big part of what I believe is articulated in the "Framework for Success in Postsecondary Writing," a document developed collaboratively by the Council of Writing Program Administrators, the National Council of Teachers of English, and the National Writing Project.*

- Writers must be curious. Writers want to know more about themselves and the world around them.

- Writers must be open. They desire answers to questions while recognizing those answers may conflict with previously held beliefs or that there may be no single answer, and the truth instead resides in shades of gray.

- Writers must be engaged. Believing what you're writing about matters—to an audience above all—makes it much easier to be involved and invested in learning.

- Writers must be creative. There is no formula for most writing, so almost every occasion involves moving from

---

* This is like the Avengers, Justice League, and X-Men coming together to solve a problem in an area of comic book superhero expertise.

what is known into the unknown and finding novel solutions to unique problems.

- Writers must be ethical and responsible. When writing to audiences, writers are responsible for the accuracy and truthfulness of what they write. Writers never knowingly deceive nor take the ideas of others without credit.

- Writers must be empathetic. Empathy not only helps us understand the audiences we're writing for but also allows us to better observe the world in which we're writing.

- Writers must be obsessive. No one will care about your own writing more than you. The desire to get it "right" starts with the writer.

- Writers must learn from their experiences. A fancy term for this is "metacognition," or thinking about thinking. This is where the reflection portion of the experiences comes in.

Think of these as the values working in the background as you make choices within the writing experiences. If you're aware of their existence, you're more likely to put them into practice.

KNOWLEDGE

Writing knowledge has two dimensions:

1. Knowledge about writing, which includes understanding all the elements of the writer's practice outlined above.

2. Knowledge concerning the subject that's being written about.

Knowledge about writing is built through a combination of study, experience, and reflection. Much of what I know about writing comes from my own experiences with writing and teaching writing. While I often read what other people say about writing, most of what I know about writing is rooted in my own experiences. This is why this book focuses on writing experiences.

Subject knowledge is acquired over time as you are exposed to more and more information. Unlike cramming for a test, where much of what you "learned" disappears not long after the exam, writing requires you to retain and utilize knowledge, making it significantly "stickier."

As much as possible, the experiences in this book are designed to encourage you to access (and then build upon) your existing subject expertise. But there are some experiences that will require you to enhance your knowledge of what you're writing about.

* * *

This first section is designed to work on some of the foundational aspects of the writer's practice, things like the writer's process, considering the audience, and reading like a writer. These foundations will be carried through the rest of the book, but in this section the experiences focus specifically on highlighting these aspects of the writer's practice.

How Do I . . . ?

(Instructions)

Try to think of a procedure or activity you're expert in. Maybe you make the perfect cup of coffee. Maybe you can sew a dress or dress a deer. Can you defeat that impossible level on some video game or tell someone how to play "When the Saints Go Marching In" on the harmonica?

Everyone has some kind of expertise they're capable of sharing with the world.

Someone else may have occasion to need that expertise.

AUDIENCE

Someone who has never done what you're telling them how to do.

However, they probably cannot and should not be a blank slate. One of the first steps will be to more deeply consider who your audience will be.

PURPOSE

The audience has a need—for a good cup of coffee, to play "When the Saints Go Marching In" on the harmonica, or whatever—and they have turned to you as an expert in helping fulfill this need.

Don't be shy about it. Be the expert you are.

PROCESS

1. Spend some time inventorying your own expertise.
What are you good at? What do you enjoy doing? What do you take pride in? Make a list.

2. Select your subject.
What one skill do you think best lends itself to this particular writing-related problem? Why have you chosen that one?

3. Plan.
A good way of preparing to write the solution to this writing-related problem is to do the action itself while taking careful notes along the way.

4. Audience analysis.
Who is your audience? We know their need (to do what you already know how to do), but what might their attitudes be toward the task? Excitement? Trepidation? Something else?

Additionally, what about their knowledge? To successfully execute the mission, what will they need to know or be able to do prior to engaging with your solution to this writing-related problem?

5. Find and analyze models.
Look for models that serve similar purposes. Stay away from ones too closely related to your own task. You don't want to risk copying, and also remember that you're the expert here. You don't want to be unduly influenced by someone else's approach, which may actually be kind of crappy.

Look at how these models are formatted and structured. How do they begin? How is the information conveyed? What techniques will you use and choices will you make in your own instructions?

6. Draft.
Doing your best to meet your audience's needs, draft your document. Use your models to help guide your approach. For our purposes, you're restricted to "text only" instructions. No diagrams or illustrations are allowed or required.

7. Test draft.
Give your draft to someone else. Ideally, you can exchange drafts with someone else engaged in the same experience so you can get a perspective on this experience from the standpoint of the audience.

If possible, have them attempt the task by following your directions while you do the same with their task. If that isn't possible, try to visualize the process while reading.

Would they be successful? Where might they be confused or even lost? Identify those sections.

Areas of confusion in need of additional clarity, as well as those elements that work well, should be specifically identified and discussed.

8. Revise draft.
Based on the feedback, as well as any additional insights gained along the way, revise the draft to improve its effectiveness. Think of your audience.

9. Edit and polish.
Even small errors can throw off an audience that's trying to follow the instructions closely. Fixable mistakes can also shake their confidence in the quality of your instructions.

REFLECT

Writing instructions using only text was probably pretty hard. What could be done differently if you had the benefit of illustrations?

Is the cliché of a picture being worth a thousand words true in this case?

Is there an even better way? Would your task be better learned by a different method? What about a video or other visual simulation? What would be the trade-off between text instructions and video instructions? When would one be more useful than the other?

Or is your task something that would best be done in a live setting, either one-on-one with you as the expert or in a class setting? How would the different atmospheres change the learning? How would your role as the expert change?

What's best? Given total freedom to craft a solution to this problem, what method would you use and why? How and why is this best for the audience? (It may even be a combination of methods.)

THE WRITING PROCESS

Sometimes when I ask people if they have a writing process, they hem and haw, and say, "Maybe?" "Sorta?" "Sometimes?"

In truth, provided you're capable of eventually producing *something*, everyone has a writing process. It may not be a particularly great process and may contain counterproductive elements, but it's still a process.

In college, under the delusion that I was most creative under maximum deadline pressure, I would wait to get started the night before an assignment was due. To fuel this last-minute process, I would secure a two-liter bottle of Coca-Cola and a two-pound bag of Peanut M&M's, and chug the soda and gobble the candy as I worked. No one would confuse my college academic record with the work of a highly dedicated and accomplished student, but it got the job done.

Except . . . there was one time when I'd finished an essay at around 4:00 a.m., early by my standards, and when I tried to go to bed, I realized my heart was threatening to pound its way out of my chest. I'd managed to nearly overdose on caffeine.

And there was that other time when I procrastinated writing a short story for a creative writing class and, as the time grew shorter and shorter and nothing came, found myself writing a story about a college student with writer's block who had a story due for class in a few hours, and I knew I was doomed, doomed, doomed.

My process tended to be to put things off as long as possible, fire out something when I had no other choice, print it out, and turn it in. I would sometimes get my papers returned and see errors that were downright embarrassing but not surprising, because I hadn't actually read the whole thing again after I typed the final word.

In the "How Do I . . . ?" experience, I semiforced you to follow a writing process. But even within that process, you likely marched to the beat of your own drummer.

Everyone has a writing process because writing *is* a process. A significant part of the writer's practice is being mindful about, and seeking to refine, one's process. The writing process consists of the following stages:

1. Prewriting

2. Drafting

3. Revision

4. Editing

5. Polishing

PREWRITING

These steps can look very different depending on what's being written. A deeply researched piece may call for weeks of work in the prewriting stage and require a detailed outline before even beginning.

The prewriting period for a poem could consist of no obvious work, like library research or an outline, but may take years. If the poet is an adult looking back on something from their childhood, all the time between the incident and the starting of the writing process could be seen as prewriting.

Procrastination is prewriting. Provisioning (Coca-Cola and Peanut M&M's) is prewriting. So is reading, research, planning, thinking. I do a significant amount of prewriting while walking the dogs or exercising, as my mind drifts to what I'm about to do.

This doesn't mean prewriting has to be haphazard, though. A planned, deliberate approach to the prewriting period helps make the drafting process go more smoothly.

DRAFTING

Once words that have some potential of winding up in the final product start hitting the page, you're drafting. Prewriting may involve writing like brainstorming or mind-mapping, but until you're intentionally working on the document, you aren't drafting.

One of the mistaken notions I often see in people developing their writing practices is a belief that you start drafting only once you've figured out what you want to say.

Instead, we should think of the drafting stage as the process of figuring out what we have to say. Writing *is* thinking.

A draft is a stage of discovery in which we should be sensitive to fresh ideas and insights. Drafting may send us back to prewriting— for additional research or brainstorming or to reconsider an outline. This is to be expected.

Drafting is a tool that allows thinking to happen. We are not recording thoughts that already exist. We are uncovering the thoughts in real time.

There is no right way to draft. Some people are tortoises, others hares. Some dart forward quickly, only to retreat to go over the previous paragraph or page (this is me). Some people write sequentially, others jump from idea to idea, not worried about how they will fit together. I have even known people who write the end first, so they know where they should be heading (though often the end changes before they get there).

As long as words are hitting the page and you are thinking, you're fine. You're drafting.

REVISION

Many students I've worked with have never engaged in a genuine revision process, instead skipping all the way to editing. This is not their fault. School often doesn't allow for a robust revision process because deadlines and production are prioritized, and time is often not sufficient.

Revision is seeing (vision) again (re-), and it is a step during which writers can think fresh about what they've done and what they're trying to do next, having learned so much in the thinking and drafting process. I often finally write my way into what I meant to say the whole time at *the end* of the initial draft. Once this happens, I have to go back and rework the piece from the beginning in order to properly reflect my new discovery.

I'm fortunate enough in my work to have time to do this. The experiences in this book are designed to allow time to revise, and to give some direction to help with a productive approach to revision.

But we should also recognize that revision is never done. Just because something has been turned in doesn't mean we can't make use of it someday or won't see something that can be improved. I will pick up this book in its finished, printed, and bound form, open to a random page, and find something I want to change.

EDITING AND POLISHING

These are two different stages, but they often happen concurrently, or overlap as we move back and forth between them.

Editing is the shaping of the writing after the ideas are essentially in place. The bulk of the thinking is over; now it's a matter of making specific language choices to highlight those ideas.

Polishing is the final touch on that process—brushing away the last bits of fluff on the finely cut garment.

* * *

Everyone's writing process is unique; there's no one right way to write.

How do you feel about your process in the "How Do I . . . ?" experience? Compare it to the process you used to write instructions for a peanut-butter-and-jelly sandwich.

What was different? What aspects of the process do you want to carry forward? What parts of your process do you think you need to work on?

Should I . . . ?

(Review)

Should I go see that movie? Should I buy that app? Should I listen to this album or go to that concert? Should I read this book, check out that museum, or eat in that new restaurant over there?

Decisions, decisions everywhere. Important decisions. Your audience needs help in making one of these decisions.

Your audience wants to know if something (music, movie, book, TV show, app, clothing, food, restaurant, concert, play, video game, etc.) is any good. They have come to you for your opinion, which they will rely upon to make their decision.

AUDIENCE

Your audience is someone your age, in roughly your circumstances, who has had similar experiences. It's not you but people similar to you—your peers.

PURPOSE

You are helping the audience make the right decision *for themselves*, which makes for an interesting challenge. On the one hand, you're going to need to be opinionated. On the other hand, you're going to also have to be informative and persuasive, telling them what they need to know about your subject to make a decision for themselves, while also arguing your point of view about your experience with your subject.

PROCESS

1. Choose your subject.
Pick something you've never experienced specifically but with which you're at least a little bit familiar. You shouldn't choose a horror movie if you've never seen a horror movie, for example. A good subject intersects with your own experience and enthusiasms, but it's important that you haven't yet experienced the specific subject itself. You want to be able to record your impressions as someone coming to it for the first time, the same way your audience will ultimately be experiencing it.

2. Find models.
Find examples of solutions to this writing-related problem. This should not be difficult. You encounter them all the time.

3. Study the models.
What kinds of information and background do your models share? How are they structured? Where is the author present in the piece of writing? On what criteria is the subject judged? How do the examples help the audience in making their decision?

4. Experience your subject.
Make sure to take good notes on your experience for use as you write your piece. Consider whether your subject should be experienced only once prior to writing or if it's the kind of subject that is best experienced multiple times prior to writing.

What are the differences in these kinds of subjects? How does this make for a different piece? What role does the audience for your piece have in these choices?

5. Analyze audience.
Be particularly thoughtful in considering the dimensions of your audience's knowledge. What do they know about your subject? What might they need to know, in your review, and when will they need to know it? When should you avoid going overboard in sharing information? (Spoiler alert! Movies.)

6. Draft.
Do your thing. It's your process. Just remember your audience and purpose.

7. Test draft.
Ideally, exchange your draft with someone else engaged in a similar experience (though writing on a different specific subject). If you don't have a test audience, you can look at your own draft and ask yourself the following questions.

After reading the review, answer the following questions without referring back to the review.

- What is the subject of the review?

- What is the reviewer's recommendation regarding the subject? Thumbs-up? Thumbs-down? Thumbs-sideways?

- What reasons or evidence does the reviewer give to support their recommendation? List as many as you can remember. Once you're done listing what you remember, go back and look at the text again and find others you don't remember. Why didn't you remember them?

- Do you have any unanswered questions about the subject? What do you wish you knew that isn't in the review?

8. *Revise.*
Revise your review, attempting to meet any missing audience needs.

- If they couldn't identify the subject of the review, why not?

- Did they receive your message regarding your recommendation?

- What about the evidence? Did they recall your most important arguments? What could you do differently to highlight what matters most?

- Have you addressed all their questions? What could or should you add to the review?

9. *Edit and polish.*
When sharing your opinions, making sure there's no obvious reason to dismiss those opinions may be useful in engaging our audience.

Read the review out loud, slowly. See if you catch mistakes you didn't see before.

REFLECT

Which part of the writing process was most time consuming? Why do you think that is?

Have you ever written a formal review before? How much time was spent figuring out the ins and outs of what a review does and how it does it?

One of the best aspects of expanding your writing experiences is that once you've done something previously unfamiliar a few times, the "moves" start to become subconscious. The cognitive load—what you have to be thinking about as you're writing—drops as your familiarity increases.

If at the beginning a new form feels like ill-fitting clothes, that's to be expected. It's a normal part of building the writer's practice.

REMIX

Now repurpose your review for another medium. It can be video, Instagram, Twitter, or whatever else you can think of.

What changes do you need to make to your review to suit this switch in medium? Why must you make those changes?

ALTERNATE REMIX

Find a review of your subject that disagrees with you. If it's someplace that allows comments, start an argument. Your goal is to win the audience over to your opinion with the superiority of your insights and evidence. What will be most persuasive for the people you're trying to convince?

READING LIKE A WRITER

One of the skills writers frequently use is "reading like a writer." This skill was employed during the last experience when you were asked to study the model reviews.

Usually, we spend most of our time reading for meaning, taking in and assessing the ideas presented in a piece of writing. We ask, "What is this saying?"

Reading like a writer changes the question from *what* to *how*, as in, "How does this say what it says?"

Reading like a writer involves asking questions of the piece of writing in order to understand what it's trying to do and how it's trying to do it.

What is it? (Genre)
Why did they write it? (Purpose)
Who wrote this? (Author's style, tone, persona)
Who is it written for? (Audience)
What is it saying? (Message)

These are the elements of the rhetorical situation. Being able to analyze the rhetorical situation of a particular text is a core skill for any reader and writer.

GENRE

"Genre" is a term we use to categorize a type of expression within a medium. Film is a medium, and romantic comedy is a genre. Music is a medium, and hip hop and jazz are genres.

A genre is defined by its characteristics: form, style, subject matter, purpose. A romantic comedy is recognized by its story—two people negotiating the difficulties of a relationship—as well as its tone and even its structure. Ninety-nine percent of romantic-comedy films share the same basic plot: couple meets, couple hates each other, couple falls in love, couple breaks up, couple gets back together.

Also, there is a montage where someone tries on hats.

Writing can be categorized by genre. Novels can be mysteries or romances or science fiction. You can tell the difference between a recipe and a poem by their structure and purposes.

The word "essay" could be used to describe a genre, but for our purposes we should consider it far too general to be helpful. There are many different types of essays. The word shares its origin with "assay," which means "to test the quality of." "Essay" itself means "to try." An essay is an attempt at something, an exploration. To know what kind of essay is being written requires deeper knowledge of why we're writing and who we're writing to.

While we want to think about genre, we don't want to fall into the trap of mistaking the general for the specific. By itself, "essay" doesn't reveal much about the specifics of a genre.

As we think about genre in our writing problems, we want to understand the specifications in order to name the category, rather than determining the category and writing to those specifications.

This is what you were asked to do with the "Should I . . . ?" assignment: to understand the characteristics that make up a particular type of writing. A review is a genre, though within the genre there's lots of room for variety, and what is being reviewed plays a significant role in that variety.

No one worries about putting spoilers in a review of a blender.

Genre doesn't tell us everything we need to know, but it's a good place to start.

And in some cases, it won't really matter if we can identify the specific genre, as long as we know how it's working and what we're trying to accomplish as we engage our audience.

PURPOSE

This is the "why" of writing.

Are you aiming to inform, instruct, persuade, entertain, challenge, inspire, or some combination of the above?

Without purpose, we can't begin to make informed choices about what to say or how to say it.

For example, a good review should be informative, entertaining, and persuasive all at the same time. Figuring out how to balance those purposes is a significant part of the challenge.

Every piece of writing has a purpose. Understanding the purpose and how that purpose is fulfilled is part of reading like a writer.

AUTHOR

In this context, we think of the author as the "unique intelligence" who created the piece of writing.

The unique intelligence is expressed through a persona, the character we perceive through the writing. In some cases, the author's persona can seem almost entirely absent. In others, it is so close that it seems to be inside our heads.

Persona can be highly formal, as in a research study, or far more informal, as in a piece of writing that puts the author's experience front and center. You may have been given many "rules" to follow in your writing, like never use "I" or contractions. Rather than seeing these as rules that apply to all writing, think of them as shortcuts to achieving an academic persona.

If you don't use "I" in the "Should I . . . ?" assignment, the review starts to sound really odd.

Persona and tone are choices governed by genre, purpose, and audience. There are no hard-and-fast rules. Determining the guidelines for a particular rhetorical situation is part of reading like a writer.

AUDIENCE

The audience is the group you're writing to or for. Different audiences may demand different approaches. For example, a lecture on the solar system would be very different for an audience of astrophysicists versus an audience of third graders.

When we consider audience, we think of them in three dimensions: their needs, their attitudes, and their knowledge.

Needs: What does your audience *need* from your piece of writing? Essentially, what is the writing being used for?

How do purpose and audience intersect? To fulfill your purpose, how must you think about your audience's needs?

How are they going to read? Quickly? Multiple times? As slowly and closely as humanly possible?

And to fulfill your audience's needs, what choices do you have to make in terms of things like structure or sourcing or language?

A review is designed to help an audience make a decision for themselves. It needs to be designed to fulfill those needs.

Attitudes: What attitudes do audiences bring to your writing? Are they hostile? Excited? Wary? Are they interested in your subject or indifferent to it?

Knowing what your audience is bringing to the experience helps you better tailor the experience to their needs. Imagine writing a review about a movie by a director whose last movie flopped. If your audience knows this, they may bring a particular preconceived attitude about the movie you're reviewing. You may be able to use that attitude as a point of comparison ("another turkey from . . .") or contrast ("a triumphant return to form for . . . ").

Knowledge: What does your audience know, or think they know, about your subject or you prior to reading your writing?

Do they have any mistaken impressions that you'll need to correct? Are there things they know that you can build upon to connect with them and enhance your message?

What do you have to include because you need them to know it? What can you exclude because they know it already?

Many of the experiences will include additional, specific insights into your audience's needs, attitudes, and knowledge, but for each experience, you will be required to make choices consistent with those elements.

MESSAGE

This is simply what you have to say combined with how you say it.

As you're already intuiting, this is clearly dependent on the other aspects of the rhetorical situation (purpose, author, audience, genre).

For example, you may want to be persuasive on a particular topic (purpose), but how to be persuasive on that topic (message) may change significantly based on different audiences. Even as you tackle the same purpose, what may be motivating for one group may be off-putting to another. Calibrating your message to your audience and purpose is both difficult and necessary. The constraints of genre may also significantly impact your message. Imagine the difference between trying to persuade in a five-thousand-word piece of writing versus a 240-character tweet.

Remember, your writing is yours. Your name is on the top, and what you have to say should reflect what you believe.

Always.

SKILLS DRILLS

In this section, the goal is to focus on some of the discrete skills that are part of the writer's practice. At the same time, practicing those skills will help develop the habits of mind writers utilize when practicing their practice.

I wish there was a good synonym for "practice," but I'm committed to the word at this point. Let's just get used to saying that you're practicing your practice.

Writers must be good observers of the world around them and be able to draw meaning from what they've experienced in a way they can put into words for the benefit of others, so we'll practice that in a very specific way in the "Who Are They?" experience.

To bring the world to life on the page, it helps to have the powers of description, which we'll practice in "Where Did You Go?"

In "You Did What?" you'll put those first two experiences together, making observations and trying to use your skills of description to convey to your audience what happened on an "adventure."

And finally, in "Is It True? Did It Really Happen?" you'll practice mining your own experiences: observing your past, considering the meaning of that past in the present, and trying to bring the past alive in the present, using your skills of description.

In each of these experiences, you will have a chance to reflect on these skills, where they come from, how they can be used, and how they can be nurtured as you gain more and more experience with writing.

You will return to these skills over and over in the other experiences in this book.

Who Are They?

(Profiling)

You can tell a lot about a person by their keys. Imagine the keys in the picture above have been left behind by a person of interest in a crime. You have been hired to do a profile of this person to better understand who they are, including their attitudes and beliefs. Assume that any identifying information that could lead the authorities to this person has been exhausted. All we have are the keys and whatever you can glean from them.

Your job here is to make observations, then draw inferences from those observations. This is how Sherlock Holmes solves his mysteries, by "seeing" things no one else can see and drawing conclusions no one else is able to.

Your next experience is to practice this method, not to solve a mystery, but to understand a person—and to see the limits of observations in drawing those conclusions.

Based on very little information, you need to try to describe a person who is a stranger to both you and your audience.

AUDIENCE

A nosy, curious person who is looking for insights into the subject of your study. Think of them as a client.

PURPOSE

The purpose of the writing is to catalog your observations and inferences in a way that will be understandable and accessible to your audience.

PROCESS

1. Observe.

Spend around ten minutes looking at the keys. Write down as many different observations as you can. Observations are directly observable facts, such as there are two regular keys and two car keys and one key chain. Don't make any judgments about these observations, simply observe. While you're observing what is there, you should also be thinking about what's absent. What sorts of things do people put on key chains that aren't here?

2. Draw inferences.

What conclusions can you draw based on your observations? Who is this person? What is their gender? What do they like? How old are they? What do they do (or not do) with their time? What are their attitudes and beliefs?

3. Extend inferences.

Based on those initial inferences, what other conclusions can you draw? What does this person do with their weekends? Who are their friends and associates? This will require speculation, but make sure it's speculation grounded in observation and earlier inferences.

4. Report findings to client.

Consider an approach and format that delivers the information in a way that will be useful to your client. Be sure to be mindful of connecting your inferences to your observations so the client can appreciate your evidence. Also, they'd probably like to know how much confidence you have in your various conclusions. What do you know? What do you suspect? What's merely possible? What's wild speculation?

Include as much information as you can that's still grounded in specific observations, as well as your level of confidence in each of these conclusions.

REFLECT

Those are my keys. What were you able to discover about me?

Your list of observations should include the obvious: There are two door keys, two car keys, a single key chain. The car keys are for a Toyota and a Fiat. The key chain says "Illinois" on it and has a logo, suggesting a team or organization.

You can also observe absences. There are no frequent-buyer cards, for example.

What sorts of inferences did you draw? What can you infer about someone with two car keys? What can you infer from the make of car on those keys?

Did you guess my gender (male) or age (mid to late forties)? Based on what? Did you infer that I went to the University of Illinois for college? If you did a little digging, you'd see that the logo on that key chain was discontinued more than ten years ago, which suggests it's more than ten years old. In fact, I bought it at my summer orientation for college in 1988. What can you infer from the fact that I've had the same keychain since 1988?

That's right, I've never lost my keys. Typing that sentence virtually guaranteed that I will now lose my keys, but it's been a good run.

I'm married, which is why I have access to two cars, one for me and one for my spouse. This also suggests that we live in a place where day-to-day life requires a car. This has not always been the case during our marriage, but it is now.

The makes of the cars may give some clue to our socioeconomic status. (Not telling, but feel free to guess.)

Did you wonder if the keys belong to someone who can carry them in a pocket because there are so few? The lack of frequent-buyer cards could be interpreted as meaning I do no shopping, which is untrue but a reasonable inference. (I'm no conspiracy theorist, but I'm not a fan of having all my information tracked and sold by corporations.)

The point isn't how close you get to successfully profiling me but instead to appreciate the process of making observations and drawing inferences. This will be a core part of any writing that requires analysis. Through this process, you can create ideas directly from your own experience.

REMIX

Look at your own keys. What sorts of *incorrect* inferences could people make about you based on correct observations of your keys? What would cause someone to make these incorrect inferences? What role would stereotyping play in their incorrect inferences?

What can be done in our observations to guard against jumping to incorrect conclusions based on stereotypes?

MAKING INFERENCES FROM OBSERVATIONS

Here is a fancy word with a fancy definition:

> Semiotics: A general philosophical theory of signs and symbols that deals especially with their function in both artificially constructed and natural languages and comprises syntactics, semantics, and pragmatics.
> —Merriam-Webster

In other, more simplified, words, the world is comprised of signs and signals that convey meaning. You read them constantly, often unconsciously. For example, how do you know how to turn on the hot water?

Hot is almost always on the left side of the sink, or colored red or signaled by a little *H* on the knob. Much of your moment-to-moment reading of signs is largely unconscious.

The "Who Are They?" experience requires acting as semiotician. It involves a process of making observations (two car keys, Illinois key chain) and drawing inferences and implications from those observations. Through the process, we create "knowledge," information and insights that weren't available prior to engaging in the process.

One of the skills in any writer's practice is to see and interpret the world around them in an effort to discover things not previously known. Acting as a kind of Sherlock Holmes type, being aware of the world and asking what different signs and signals mean, will be a part of just about any writing experience.

In writing the review for the "Should I . . . ?" assignment, you may have had to make observations and draw inferences. You may have interpreted something's meaning, or its quality, by interpreting your own observations.

But as the remix for the previous assignment demonstrates, stereotyping and something called "confirmation bias"—where we see something we expect to see—are always potential threats. Guarding against them requires practicing one particular writer's habit of mind: openness.

Many of us will make judgments about a person's character based on their clothing or appearance, and sometimes that may be accurate, but often we are succumbing to stereotypes, failing to look at the signals closely and critically and to guard against knee-jerk assumptions. Being able to revise an initial impression is a vital writing skill rooted in openness as a habit of mind.

Where Did You Go?

(Sense Memory)

I am about to put you inside a time machine and, with a mere two words, send you to a different time and place.

For it to work you have to prepare your mind, though. Get comfortable and clear away any distractions. All you need is this book.

Once you're ready, I'll ask you to turn the page, which will put you inside the time machine. You will be briefly transported out of the present and into the past. How long you stay in the past is up to you. Once you're back in the present, or if for some reason the time machine misfires, turn the page again, where we'll rejoin the experience.

Are you ready? Mind clear? Comfortable?

You sure?

Okay. Turn the page.

Cinnamon rolls.

Did you go somewhere? Where? What did you experience when you were transported? What sensations were present?

Lots of people tell me they travel to an airport with the smell of Cinnabon wafting through the air. Others go to a holiday morning in the house they grew up in. If cinnamon rolls didn't work for you, let's try again. Even if they did work, let's try again. Turn the page when you're ready.

Fried chicken.

Those words are triggering a "sense memory," with smell being a particularly powerful way of evoking an experience from the past that's been stored away in your brain, almost always without a conscious effort on your part. On occasion, you will hear people liken our brains to computers, and often the way we're asked to learn reflects this view: we're required to read, retain, and retrieve information.

But the metaphor of brain as computer does not reflect what we know about our neurobiology, nor does it connect to how we exist in the world. Humans are wired as "interaction" machines, arriving on the scene with a dozen or more reflexive responses to stimuli. Our brains are constantly doing all kinds of things we're not aware of, squirreling experiences away where we may never access them again, unless triggered, often subconsciously.

Actors use sense memory as a way to evoke emotion in a scene. By recalling a time when they felt an emotion similar to what they're attempting to portray, they can more believably embody that emotion in the moment.

Writers can use sense memory as a way to access material that may help us bring a particular experience alive. It is a way of getting in touch with some of these subconscious, hidden parts of ourselves, and reminding us we contain much more possibility than we can consciously access at any given moment.

This experience is different from most every other experience in the book in that it is asking you to write not for anyone but yourself. You are going to get in a time machine, triggered by a song, in an attempt to remember what you never realized you knew.

AUDIENCE

You are the audience. This is meant as a pure experience with no product to be consumed by others at the end of the process. I'm not even sure what to call what you'll be writing. You're trying to capture a memory.

PROCESS

Read the full process before starting the experience.

1. Locate a memory.

Get comfortable, have handy some way to write down whatever is going to come to you, and start listening to music you know and love on shuffle. As you listen to the first few seconds of a song, see if you are transported to the time and place when you first heard that song. If so, move on to step 2. Just keep flipping until something hits you. If nothing is happening, take a break, go do something else to clear your mind, and come back and try again later.

2. Re-experience the memory.

Once the memory hits, try to follow it back into the moment evoked by the song. There will be both physical and emotional dimensions to the memory. You will likely be able to remember what you saw, smell, touched, and tasted in the moment evoked by this music. Perhaps not all the senses will be present, but some will be, and as you follow the memory more sensations will arrive.

Only those of us past a certain vintage can appreciate this one, but those raised during the 8-track era may recall that there is a part in the live version of Marvin Gaye's "Got to Give It Up" where the music fades out, the track switches, and the song fades back in. When I listen to the song today, and the part where the fade would happen, I am transported to the "way back" seat in my parents' station wagon, a 1976 Oldsmobile Vista Cruiser, where I am feeling vaguely nauseous from the exhaust fumes as I ride facing backward, looking out the rear window.

I could do this all day, but this isn't about me.

As you experience the memory, record what you're experiencing, focusing on the sense details and emotions of the moment. You'll know it's going well as you lose touch with present reality and venture deeper into the memory, as more and more associations arrive, perhaps even triggering a chain of memories, one after the other. Just follow that flow for as long as you can.

3. File away your re-experienced memory.

Whatever you capture, make sure to find a home for it where you can go back to it later. Right now, it's raw material. Think of it as lumber that could be used to build anything you like when the time is right.

REFLECT

If you were able to really get into experiencing a memory, and lost track of the present, my question is, "What's up with that?" What did that feel like? Was it different from other times when you're writing or concentrating?

You may have been in a moment of what psychologist Mihaly Csikszentmihalyi has conceptualized as "flow," which he describes this way: "The best moments in our lives are not the passive, receptive, relaxing times. . . . The best moments usually occur if a person's body or mind is stretched to its limits in a voluntary effort to accomplish something difficult and worthwhile."

Writers are often in the pursuit of flow, a depth of engagement in which ideas and language arrive without knowing where they're coming from. At its best, a state of flow can almost trigger a physical buzzing sensation in my head, like a high.

It is difficult to access and even harder to maintain. I have many days of work when I never achieve flow, even as I seek it out. But the more familiar you become with the sensation, and how you can trigger your own engagement, the better for your writing practice.

Writing is thinking, and flow is a period of extremely elevated thinking that hardly feels like you're thinking at all.

REMIX

Make a playlist to represent and honor a period in your life. It can be a good period or a bad period, but either way choose some songs, list them, and include a brief descriptions for each, explaining why it's included and what it represents from the period. If you like, you can publish your list on a streaming service or any other appropriate outlet.

BRINGING THE WORLD TO THE PAGE

Pop quiz. Please give each of the following words a numerical value that expresses how many times out of one hundred something must happen if we are to use the word to describe the frequency of its happening.

In other words, we're looking for a percentage. For example, if something happens "all the time," how often does it happen, expressed as a percentage?

Answers are on the next page. Don't peek.

1. Most   3. Few   5. Never
2. Many   4. A majority   6. Always

ANSWERS

Despite almost everyone knowing what these words mean, there are no specific, concrete answers to the question I posed. When I do this live and ask people to tell me how often something happens if it happens "most of the time," I've received answers ranging from ten to ninety. "Few" has been as few as three and as many as forty.

Even "never" and "always," seemingly straightforward in their meaning, never (hah!) draw universal responses. Sure, in theory "never" means "never," as in zero percent of the time, but we often use "never" to mean something else.

YOU NEVER TAKE OUT THE GARBAGE!

In the sentence above, "never" means something like "I take out the garbage more often than you, and I'm upset about that fact."

By themselves, all the words in the quiz are abstractions, dependent on context for meaning, and even with context they're sometimes open to interpretation. This doesn't make the words useless, but we should understand the limits of abstractions.

"Beautiful" is another abstract word, as reflected in the cliché, "Beauty is in the eye of the beholder." Anyone would be pleased to be called beautiful, but if we wrote something like "A beautiful horse appeared on the horizon," we haven't done much to paint a concrete picture of that horse.

The degree of specificity depends on what effects we would like to achieve. If I say, "Picture a dog," my audience is likely picturing many different dogs. Most people think of their own dog.

If I say "big dog," the list of possible dogs narrows. "Big black dog" and about half are thinking of a black Lab. "Little black dog with a graying muzzle and dabs of white on his toes and a slightly wonky right eye." I've just described one of my dogs, Truman.

The sense-memory, time-travel experience is an example of how describing an experience through sense details can help bring something alive with specifics. Next, the adventure report, "You Did What?" is a chance to engage this part of the writer's practice more purposefully.

You Did What?

(Adventure Report)

In this experience, you're going to have an adventure and then write about it.

An adventure is doing anything you would not do in the normal course of your day-to-day life. Seeing a movie is not an adventure. Horseback riding may be an adventure, unless you're a rodeo rider or cowpoke.

An adventure need not, and in this case should not, be physically dangerous. I assigned this in a class once, and a student's adventure was trying to jump over a moving car. (He had ambitions to be a Hollywood stuntman one day.) He cleared the hood but hit the windshield, breaking it and his arm.

Don't do that. Whether something is an adventure depends on the individual having it. It could be adventurous to ride an elevator for a couple of hours facing the other people in the cab rather than the elevator doors.

Whatever adventure you choose, just make sure it will not do physical or emotional harm to you or anyone else. There are plenty of adventures to be had without doing damage.

AUDIENCE

The audience is interested in hearing about your adventure. They bring an initial curiosity to your report, but that doesn't mean their curiosity extends all the way to the end.

Your job is to make your adventure come alive for the audience. You're not going to tell them what you did. You're going to show them.

PROCESS

1. Choose an adventure.
Again, it doesn't need to be life changing or earth shattering, just something you haven't done before that you'd like to do.

2. Have the adventure.
Resist the urge to capture the experience in photos or video. When you're taking photos or video, you're taking photos or video, not having the experience. Try to be as present and aware as possible during the adventure. Take in the experience.

Immediately after your adventure, you'll want to capture the sensory experience of the adventure in your notes. What did you see, smell, taste, touch, and hear on your adventure? What was it like? (Consider metaphors that may describe your adventure.) How did the adventure make you feel?

Sometimes it helps to write these impressions down in a rush, not worrying about sentences or grammar but simply trying to put yourself back in the experience and to capture the sensations for later consideration. No one but you will ever see or care about this part of the process.

3. Write an adventure report.

A journalistic—who, what, where, when, why—approach to writing the adventure often works well, though you will want to be mindful about how you answer these questions, the order, the length, and the detail. Your goal is to engage the reader with the story of your adventure enough to get them to read to the end.

Think about making the adventure come alive on the page by using the sense details you captured in your notes. It will likely take a couple of drafts to get the report down and polish it to the highest possible shine. Length matters here. You want to capture the adventure without blabbering on too long.

4. Share your adventure report.

Find a reader. If you can, find five or ten readers. Have them read the report once, and when they're done ask them to respond to the following questions:

1. On a scale of one to ten, where one means it was similar to slogging through foot-deep mud, five equals meh, and ten means it reminded you of what it must be like to effortlessly fly through the sky on the back of the winged horse Pegasus, how did you feel as you were reading this report?

2. After finishing the report, without looking back at it, what's the most memorable scene, image, or part of the experience? What stands out in your mind in hindsight?

REFLECT

What part or parts of your adventure report do your readers recall after reading? What "sticks"? What details are most likely to stand out in their minds? Was there a common thread in the responses? What explains the stickiness of certain parts? What role do the sense details play?

If nothing was particularly sticky, why do you think this was the case? What could be done to enhance the stickiness?

REMIX

Rewrite your adventure, only this time as a script for a thirty-second ad attempting to "sell" people on taking the same adventure. Even if you don't recommend people repeating your adventure, for the purposes of this experience you must pretend it's not only worth doing but people would really be missing out if they didn't try it.

If you're not familiar with the format for a commercial script—and odds are you aren't—you should avail yourself of the many on-line resources that will give you templates for how it should look.

Is It True?
Did It Really Happen?

(Experience vs. Memory)

The writer Wright Morris said, "Anything processed by memory is fiction."

This seems true. Our memories are not perfect recording devices. I have memories of things from my childhood my family members swear never happened.

We are also governed by what psychologist Daniel Kahneman identifies as the tug-of-war between our "experiencing self" and our "remembering self."

Our experiencing self is us when we're living our moment-to-moment lives. Most of our experiences pass without notice or triggering any kind of memory to be stored for later. Daniel Kahneman says our "remembering self" is a "storyteller" who prioritizes moments that disrupt or alter the narrative of the experience.

Additionally, we have a bias toward weighting the ends of experiences. Just about everyone has experienced a movie they were enjoying up until a disappointing ending, after which they declare the movie to "suck," even though they might have approved of eighty-five of its ninety minutes.

You could have a pair of identical vacation experiences during which everything was perfect, except you lost your wallet one time at the beginning of the vacation and the other at the end. Only the one when you lost it at the end will be recalled unfavorably.

Marriages that end in divorce are remembered as misery, but it's clear this couldn't have been true for the entire duration of the marriage.

In this writing experience, you're going to reconsider an experience from your life and see if it alters your perception of the experience.

AUDIENCE

While it's likely the results of this writing experience will be of interest to others, the primary audience is yourself. This is an experience of personal reflection. You never know when it may prove useful for some other piece of writing, but for now it's all for you.

Writing can be that way sometimes.

PROCESS

1. Choose experience.
Think about an experience from your life for which you harbor either mixed or negative feelings. It could be a class, a relationship, a vacation, a job, an apartment—anything.

2. Remember your experiences.
Daniel Kahneman's research suggests that most of our experiences never take root in our memories, but a careful reconsideration will help give a fuller perspective of this experience.

If it's something like a vacation, try to recall the entire trip, not just the part that went poorly, such as being stuck on the "It's a

Small World" ride at Disney World when a power cut knocked out everything except the ride's soundtrack, which repeated endlessly for six hours.

Walk yourself through the full experience. Were there times that were good, when you were happy and fulfilled?

3. Write the story of your experience.
Get down as much as you recall while going through this active remembering process. Does it change how you view the experience?

One of the most important implications of Kahneman's research is that our remembering selves impact our happiness. We're very good at remembering the bad things and less good at remembering the low-grade or unremarkable positive things.

People who can "live in the moment" tend to report being happier on a day-to-day basis compared to those of us who spend time looking to the past or the future.

What have you discovered about your memory?

REFLECT

Writing itself often falls prey to the divide between the experiencing self and remembering self.

Students will decide whether a writing experience was worthwhile based on the grade. Too many disappointing grades make students believe writing just isn't worth it.

I have worked on many "failed" projects in my life, including entire drafts of books that proved unpublishable. I often look back on those disappointments with a certain amount of bitterness,

thinking I must've wasted any time spent on them since they ultimately didn't pan out.

And yet I can remember moments of working on those books
when I had great days of writing and it all felt really good. I also
tend to forget bad days on projects that ultimately sold to publishers, because those efforts had a happy ending.

I now try to make a conscious effort to be more aware of the experience of writing and not judge how I'm doing by the results. I
find this makes it much easier and more pleasant to write, which
results in me writing more, which results in me writing better—a
kind of virtuous circle.

How do you tend to view your work? Is it only worth it if it pays
off? Do you enjoy the journey no matter what the result might be?
Or is it some kind of balance between the two?

What conditions help you do your best work?

ANALYTICAL WRITING

Consider what makes up a good conversation in everyday life.

For a good conversation, it helps if the parties involved are both interested and well versed in the topic. It helps if they're listening to each other, understanding the message they're receiving, and then responding in appropriate ways that move the conversation forward.

Good conversations tend to flow, moving from topic to topic, as fresh insights are uncovered and the participants add on to each other's ideas in an effort to bring a little more light and sense to whatever is being discussed.

Now imagine a conversation where there is an additional party, an interested, listening audience.

I want us to think of the analytical experiences in this next section as conversations because writing is communication. In this case, we're using the vehicle of the conversation as a way to convey meaning to our interested listening (or reading, in this case) audience.

The goal in these conversations is to leave the audience smarter and better informed.

In the first experience in this section, "What's the Right Thing to Do?," you'll tackle an ethical dilemma. Your goal is not to simply answer the question but to discuss it in such a way that your audience has a better understanding of the depths and complexities of the ethical dilemma.

Next you'll go deep into trying to understand and explicate a conspiracy theory by answering the question, "If It Isn't True, Why Do People Believe It?" Why do we tend to believe certain things, even when the evidence points in a different direction? What kinds of biases may color our perceptions of the world?

"Who Are We?" and "What's So Funny?" are conversations about "texts." You will help the audience uncover meaning that isn't apparent at first glance but once revealed will advance the depth of conversation about those texts.

The final three experiences, "What's Going to Happen?," "How's It All Going to End?," and "What If . . . ?" go deep with your skills at drawing inferences from observations, in this case doing analysis on events that have yet to, and may never, occur.

There are no absolutely right answers to these questions, but there are answers that can be seen by the audience to be correct. To achieve this kind of connection with your audience means committing to the idea of engaging in a conversation that leaves your audience better off than they were before, while utilizing all aspects of the writer's practice to the best of your abilities.

What's the Right Thing to Do?

(Ethical Dilemma)

When's the last time you made a choice that involved an ethical dilemma?

Maybe we should first agree on what makes an ethical dilemma. Which of the following is best viewed as an ethical dilemma?

Deciding whether or not to show up to your job.
Deciding whether or not to drive the speed limit.
Deciding whether or not to recycle a plastic bottle.

I had a teacher tell me once that an easy way to know you're in the midst of an ethical dilemma is that you have to determine right from wrong when no one is looking. This has always made sense to me.

Showing up at your job is not an ethical dilemma, because if you don't show up, you don't get paid, and if you don't show up often enough, you won't have a job any longer.

The speed limit sometimes feels like an ethical dilemma, given that most of us tend to exceed the limits by at least a little bit, but the limit is ultimately enforceable by law.

On the other hand, provided you don't actively litter, there is no such thing as the recycling police. We're perfectly free to harm the earth by throwing a plastic bottle into the garbage to wind up in a landfill, where it will reside for the next ten thousand years (I'm guessing).

In this experience, I'm going to provide an ethical dilemma for you to solve in two different ways.

THE DILEMMA

Imagine your friend Sally works in the admissions office of an elite university. It's her job to compile the data that will be used by a prominent magazine in its annual rankings of colleges and universities. The stats she compiled make it look like her school may decline in the rankings. While everyone agrees that the rankings are largely meaningless as a reflection of the quality of education a school provides, they are a popular topic in the media, and slipping in the ranks may cause a decrease in alumni donations or lead to fewer people applying, which may cause an additional decline in the rankings the following year.

Sally's boss wants her to change the numbers in order to prevent the school from declining in the rankings.

Sally comes to you for advice regarding her dilemma.

Write answers to two different questions.

1. After hearing Sally describe the situation, what do you tell her she should do? Why are you recommending she do this?

2. What's the ethically correct thing to do, and why is it the ethically correct thing to do?

AUDIENCE

The audience is someone who is interested in understanding more about how people navigate ethical dilemmas. Your purpose isn't to portray yourself as ethical or honest or superknowledgeable about ethics. Your job is to describe, as best you can, what decision you would make and why, and then to describe the most ethical course, presuming these two answers are not the same. If they are the same, spend some time explaining why.

The audience is not interested in judging your decision or calibrating your ethical compass. This is a fact-finding mission about how and why people make decisions in the real world.

PROCESS

1. Decide what you'd recommend.

Often, it helps to just go with your gut. Most of us aren't even fully aware when we're confronted by an ethical dilemma, and rarely pause to reflect on the ethics of a decision, so whatever it is you first think you're likely to recommend is probably what you would tell Sally.

In a piece of writing, describe that decision and the thinking that underpins that decision. Your audience is most interested in the "why" of your decision, so make sure you engage in a thorough discussion of how you wound up making your recommendation, even if it is based on your gut.

In other words, show your work.

2. Analyze the ethics.

You've described what you think you would recommend, now consider what other alternatives Sally could consider. What are the different actions she could take under this scenario? List as many different actions as you can think of.

Another way of breaking down the ethics of a situation is to identify the different stakeholders in a given situation. Who are all the interested parties to this dilemma?

Think of anyone who may be impacted by this scenario.

Looking at the different possible choices, and considering the different stakeholders, what is the most ethical choice in the above scenario?

3. Explain the ethics.

In another piece of writing, explain why what you've identified as the most ethical choice is indeed the most ethical choice. This may involve comparing and contrasting your recommendation to Sally with other possible choices and arguing why another path may be the most ethical. Or if you believe your recommendation to Sally is the most ethically correct decision, explain why you're recommending this, as well as the possible consequences for Sally if she follows your recommendation.

4. Revise, edit, polish.

Make sure both pieces are as thoroughly and clearly expressed as you can manage. They will stand alone because you won't be around to explain what you "really" meant. Revise and edit them with your audience and purpose in mind.

REFLECT

Like most ethical dilemmas, there's a bit of a gray area here. On the one hand, the rankings themselves aren't truly reflective of the quality of Sally's institution, and for the institution to be harmed based on meaningless data seems bad. Plus, Sally is being asked—maybe even ordered—to do this by her boss. Imagine that Sally refuses but her boss changes the data anyway. Is Sally absolved of any responsibility?

On the other hand, they would be fudging the numbers, putting incorrect data into the world that would be publicly available. The real data is presumably accessible somewhere.

How you decide the ethics of this situation depends on how you view the different issues and the different stakeholders (Sally, her boss, the school, current students, potential students, administration, the magazine) in the equation.

One could argue that the *most* ethical act is to not only refuse the boss's order, but also to blow the whistle if the wrong numbers are put forward publicly. What might the consequences for Sally be if she took this route?

It's tricky.

Is there a gap between what you would tell Sally to do and what you believe is the ethical thing to do? Why? What are the barriers preventing people in this particular case from acting ethically? Are there different gradations of ethical behavior?

Finally, consider the same scenario, only look at it through the lens of a long view rather than the immediate consequences. Let's say Sally changes the numbers, and something similar happens the next year and she's confronted with the same dilemma, only this time the reported numbers bear even less resemblance to reality?

Some of this may boil down to individual character, but my experience is many "good" people would still have a hard time doing the ethical thing in this kind of scenario. Doing the right thing often seems to carry risks that doing the wrong thing doesn't.

Why?

REMIX

Write your own ethical dilemma. Make it a hard one, both for people to feel like they'd do the ethical thing, as well as being complicated in terms of examining the ethics.

TITLES

Thus far, I've been ignoring titles, but that's not because they're unimportant.

Sometimes a title may be purely utilitarian, like titling a memo or the minutes to a meeting. In this case, the titles merely need to communicate some very straightforward facts about what the audience will find underneath the title.

But other times the title has to do a lot of work.

Titles are the writer's first foot forward, the introduction to the audience, akin to a handshake when you meet someone new. A handshake can't be so great that it will override other character flaws, but a bad handshake can be difficult to overcome.

A bad or even so-so title could be worse than a bad handshake; if the title doesn't sufficiently intrigue, the audience may not read further. Writing in school, where a teacher is required to read whatever we turn in, distorts the reality that in the real world audiences are under no such obligation.

I learned this lesson the first time I had a short story accepted for publication, a very exciting time following a zero-for-two-hundred start to my career when it came to submitting my work to literary journals.

The only thing was the editor who accepted the story told me I needed to change the title. I had submitted the story under the title "Stillness," and he politely told me that no one is going to rush to read a short story titled "Stillness." (Perhaps my bad titling explains some of that bad start to my publishing career.)

He gave me the weekend to come up with a better title. Nothing was coming from the story itself, but that weekend my wife and I had an appointment to take our two young nieces to the circus, and that's where I found my title.

You know the circus, right? Like Ringling Brothers and Barnum & Bailey, now defunct, but back then a three-ring spectacle taking place in a ten-thousand-seat arena, with lions and tigers and acrobats and guys driving motorcycles around the inside of a large metal ball.

This was not that kind of circus. This was a traveling circus of the kind that puts in for a couple of days at the county fairground and your grocery store offers free tickets with a ten-dollar purchase. It was a one-ring circus, with a ringmaster in a filthy-looking coat and tails who did a snake charming routine with an albino python that was either made out of rubber or dead.

The children loved it, of course, because children are easily fooled, but I found the whole thing pretty grim, until the finale, the parade of elephants, when it went past grim to existentially depressing.

The parade was only two elephants long, the one behind holding the tail of the one in front with its trunk. I noticed the one in front had two dark streaks running from its eyes, as though it had been crying. I'm sure it was something bad, like conjunctivitis, or an infection, but in a bolt a title popped into my head, "The Circus Elephants Look Sad Because They Are."

Did it have anything to do with the story—an odd tale of a man who goes to an interview with a career counselor who is a former

UFC fighter (from the days when hair pulling was allowed) and who threatens to steal the man's wife from him? Not really, by which I mean not at all.

But it was odd and would draw attention, the only purpose of a title for a short story by a writer who had never previously been published and desperately wanted attention. If anyone ever asked, I could make up some rationale for it reflecting the spirit of despair with which my protagonist lives. (No one ever asked.)

It worked. When the journal it appeared in was reviewed in a couple of places, my story was specifically mentioned. When I put the title in cover letters accompanying subsequent submissions of stories to other journals, editors would recognize it, and maybe I looked a little like a somebody.

I've paid a lot of attention to titles since then. The proper title for this book has been a subject of discussion, with a good dozen people weighing in. I hope we picked the right one.

A good title gets attention, but it also must be appropriate to the audience and occasion. Think about how disappointing Internet clickbait titles are when they lure you in with promises of amazing things and you find nothing special.

Titles will be part of every experience going forward. Be mindful, consider how examples of the types of thing you're writing do it, and don't just slap something on at the last moment.

You don't want the equivalent of one of those "here's a dead fish for you" handshakes as a title.

If It Isn't True,
Why Do People Believe It?

(Conspiracy Theory Analysis)

Every generation has its urban legends, stories everyone believes. For my generation (Gen X), a commonly held urban legend is that Mikey, a character from a commercial for Life cereal, died from eating Pop Rocks mixed with soda.

This did not happen, though it'd be kind of awesome if it did. Not awesome for Mikey, obviously, or his loved ones, but just a great story, you know?

In recent years, I have heard students at two different universities tell me they're certain the cafeteria staff puts laxatives in the food as a way to prevent food poisoning under the theory that the faster the food moves through one's system the less likely one is to contract E. coli. For this to be true, we would have to believe cafeterias are deliberately poisoning students in order to keep from poisoning students.

We also have a related phenomenon called the Mandela Effect, in which large groups of people collectively remember something that never happened. It's named after South African civil rights leader Nelson Mandela, who millions of people remember dying in jail during the apartheid era (1948–91) in that country, when in reality he lived to see the end of apartheid and become president of South Africa before dying at age ninety-five in 2013.

Other examples of the Mandela Effect include people believing the song "We Are the Champions" by Queen ends with the words "of the world" (it doesn't), and that Chick-fil-A was once spelled Chic-fil-A or Chik-fil-A (it wasn't). (If you search for the Mandela Effect on the Internet, you'll see dozens of other examples.)

One theory explaining the Mandela Effect is that multiple universes run through time concurrently, and we occasionally "slip" between them, temporarily experiencing one of the other timelines before slipping back to our main timeline. It's a cool idea, based in genuine theoretical physics, but honestly I find it a little disappointing. If I can slip into an alternate universe, I'd prefer one where I can jump like thirty feet in the air, rather than one where Chick-fil-A is spelled differently.

Anyway, if we set aside the parallel universe theory, there's usually a rational explanation for why so many people have mistaken memories. In the case of Nelson Mandela's death, I believe it's likely people are conflating Mandela with Bantu Stephen Biko, another prominent South African civil rights activist, who tragically did die in jail in 1977, having been beaten by police. Biko's story was prominent in the news at the time and further popularized by a movie, *Cry Freedom* (1987), starring Denzel Washington as Biko. Over time, as Mandela came to represent the fight against apartheid in so many people's minds, I believe he became *the* avatar for the struggle. Anything that happened to a South African civil rights leader must have happened to Mandela.

When examined, any urban legend, including examples of the Mandela Effect, tells us something about the culture in which it thrives, as well as why people believe the legends.

EXPERIENCE

Using an urban legend as a jumping-off point, explore the legend and develop a theory as to why it is believed by so many people, while also convincingly debunking the legend.

AUDIENCE

You're writing for someone who believes the urban legend to be true, with the purpose of convincing them it isn't true and explaining what is actually true.

Consider how difficult this might be. It's possible you will be slaughtering someone else's sacred cow, or challenging something they're certain they remember happening. This can be unsettling. No one likes to be told they're wrong. There's a reason so many of these legends persist. In many cases people *want* to believe them.

You'll have to do a thorough analysis of the audience's needs, attitudes, and knowledge in order to devise an approach to achieving your goal. You'll probably have to revisit those thoughts throughout your process, to make sure you're not unintentionally alienating them in ways that will prevent them from appreciating your message.

PROCESS

1. Choose an urban legend.
It can be fun to first try to think of something you believe to be true, but on second thought may be an urban legend. For a decade, I assumed that Mikey of Life cereal died from eating Pop Rocks, because I'd heard it somewhere and didn't bother to question it.

The legend need not be something trivial or silly. That we're supposed to drink eight glasses of water a day to stay healthy is not backed by any scientific evidence. In some cases it may be actively harmful by overtaxing the kidneys. Go ahead, look it up for yourself. There are hundreds of these sorts of things floating around. It can start to get a little spooky once you recognize how much you think you know is based in . . . not much.

2. Investigate.
Find out as much as you can about the urban legend you've chosen. Many of them will be debunked by a single website (such as Snopes .com), but don't settle for one account. You're looking to surround the problem, including by finding whatever evidence you can that indicates the urban legend might be true (or the origins of why so many people believe it may be true).

3. Figure out what you think you want to say.
Different writers will do different things in this step. Some like to do lots of brainstorming and/or outlining. Others like to arrange their research as they look for inspiration. Personally, I usually just start writing. I grab onto a single idea, write until I've exhausted it, and hope and pray another idea appears. I often don't even know what I'm writing; I'm just trying to uncover the ideas. It's my version of brainstorming.

4. Draft.
Keeping your purpose in mind, write a draft. Remember that it's an argument with a particular purpose, to convince your audience that a particular urban legend is not true. Length? Whatever—it's a draft. Write until you've exhausted what you have to say about your subject. We call this a "down draft," where you get it all down.

5. *Shape the writing.*

Looking at all the material you've generated, and considering your audience's needs, attitudes, and knowledge, shape what you've done into a coherent essay that fulfills the purpose of debunking the legend while also offering insight into why the legend is so persistent, and doing it in a way that will convince those who were previously inclined to believe the legend.

As for structure, think of your audience. Each step of the way, they will have needs you should seek to meet. You may shock them in the beginning in a way that will make them resist the rest of your message, which means you should then attend to that shock and reassure them they'll be better off knowing the truth. A different approach may involve walking them through the evidence bit by bit to induce them to come to the conclusion you're advocating for essentially on their own.

I can't tell you the best structure, because it is highly dependent on your choice of legend and your audience. Tone is going to matter too. If you come across as a know-it-all, or seem dismissive of anyone who might've believed the legend, you're fighting an uphill battle.

Length? Long enough, and not a sentence longer.

6. *Get feedback.*

This is a piece of writing that will probably benefit from getting feedback from other people. To help them, develop some questions you want them to answer about the piece. Without specific questions, readers may just tell you something is good or not good. What do you want your readers to consider about your writing?

7. Revise, edit, polish.
When you're trying to be convincing, making the piece as polished as possible is usually a sound idea.

8. Title.
A title that invites the reader in, to explore what you've found, and opens them up to learning something new feels like the right move here. Good titles sometimes show up unbidden, but sometimes they take some coaxing.

REFLECT

Reflect on the feedback portion of this experience. How helpful was the feedback to improving your piece? What was helpful? What wasn't helpful? In hindsight, would you have given your readers different questions to focus on?

Imagine yourself on the other side of the equation, reading someone else's piece written with the same purpose in mind. What would you do to try to be helpful to them?

Who Are We?

(Rhetorical Analysis of a Commercial)

Imagine an alien race has been collecting intelligence about Americans entirely through a single medium: television commercials.

Based on television commercials, what would this alien species know about us? Given the prevalence of ads for pharmaceuticals, they'd have to think we were awfully frail. We must also hold something called "beer" in extremely high esteem.

What if we take a closer look at a single television commercial and ask what it says about us as a culture? Sure, commercials are used to sell stuff, but they sell us stuff by reflecting aspects of our culture to us.

In every commercial, there is the surface text: "Buy this because of these reasons."

There is also subtext. This is what's underneath the text, the underlying cultural connections that help sell the product.

We read subtexts all the time without thinking about it as our subconscious semiotician kicks in. One of the things I had to learn when I moved to the South is that saying "bless her heart" about someone can actually be an insult. Social expectations dictate that you're not allowed to insult someone directly, so it's done through subtext. If you don't understand the subtext, it can be very confusing.

One of the consistent subtexts of American commercials is that work is miserable and the only relief one gets from that misery is partying (when you're young) or family (when you're older).

A Corona Light commercial from 2012 named "Stan" is an example of the former.

In the spot, a young man who looks to be a relatively recent college graduate goes through his daily routine. A monotone singsong chant of "Stan, Stan, eat, work, gym, shower, beer, watch, sleep" plays as a series of still shots representing each of the words cycles through on-screen. Sometimes "bar" replaces "beer," and he also occasionally dreams (accompanied by a picture of a sheep), but overall Stan's life seems to be pure drudgery.

Until Corona Light shows up, and all of a sudden it's all "bro hugs, costume party, girl, karaoke, dance-a-thon, photo booth, digit swapping, all night." The pictures show Stan having fun, including with the same young woman in the photo booth, staying up all night after having swapped digits, suggesting perhaps Stan has found companionship.

The spot ends with the tagline "A Refreshing Change of Beer," as though getting one's beer right is the key to happiness.

Occasionally beer is seen as a reward after a hard day, but more often—as in a famous and award-winning ad for Bud Light called "Swear Jar," in which office workers swear constantly in order to fill a "swear jar" with proceeds that will be used to purchase Bud Light—beer is the thing that liberates us from our terrible workaday lives.

While the commercials are advertising beer, they are also selling an idea that Americans are expected to actively dislike their jobs. Personally, I find this distressing. If at all possible, people should like their jobs, especially considering the fact that during a given week many of us will spend more time working than doing anything else other than sleeping.

This kind of cultural reinforcement becomes cyclical; the commercial text is born out of the culture and in turn reinforces the culture it was born from.

Your task in this experience is to engage in a process of observation, analysis, and synthesis in an effort to uncover what a single commercial says about American culture.

AUDIENCE

Your audience is interested in looking deeper into our experiences of the world and being shown something they didn't initially recognize. They have seen the commercial at least once but don't have it memorized or anything like that.

PROCESS

1. Choose a commercial.
I'm showing my age by calling them television commercials, since they're now viewable anywhere videos are available. A thirty-second ad is best. It gives you enough material to work with, without being overwhelmed.

2. Process the text.
You should employ my not-yet-patented ROAS (react, observe, analyze, synthesize) method, which is also discussed in the "What's So Funny?" experience.

React: Watch the commercial. How do you respond? Is it persuasive? Do you have an emotional response to the surface text about what they're trying to sell you? What are you reacting to?

Observe: Look more closely and make specific observations. Most commercials have a narrative element in which they're telling a kind of story. What's the story of your commercial? What sorts of scenes and images are shown? Who is in the ad? What do the people in the ad look like? How would you describe them in terms of demographics (age, gender, race, etc.) and personality?

You're looking for enough material to ultimately do your analysis and synthesis, which will take the form of an argument about the subtext of the ad.

Analyze: Put these observations together in order to answer some questions. Who is the ad targeting? Why? How do you know? What is important or valuable in the world of the ad? (The "Stan" ad values a generic kind of partying fun.) What would be viewed as good and bad in the world of the ad?

Synthesize: This is what will happen as you draft. You should feel like you have a bunch of raw material, but you might not be sure how it all fits together. That's good. Think of your synthesis like you're building a house and your observations and analysis are the building materials.

The only wrinkle is that you're building the house without a full blueprint. If you're an outliner, you might want to do some of that work here.

3. Write a discovery draft.

Using the raw material, write your synthesis, which uncovers the ad's subtext for the benefit of the audience. While you're writing, you should be engaging in audience analysis, asking yourself what questions they will have and then answering them at the appropriate moments.

It makes sense to start the piece with a description of the ad that helps increase the audience's familiarity with the text. After that, what do you think you should tell them to help them appreciate your message?

4. Process your draft.

What's your message? Where is it? Do you have sufficient evidence to support your argument and analysis?

What audience questions does each paragraph or section answer? List them. Does the flow make sense?

5. Revise.

Here's where your attention to the audience really matters. Are you telling them something about the ad that isn't immediately apparent? You want the sensation of pulling back a veil and allowing them to see the subtext, which was always there but they didn't recognize until you showed it to them.

If you recognize that you've discovered something about the ad you didn't know before, you're probably going to do the same for them.

6. Edit, polish, title.

Are you describing the ad with as much precision and concision as you can manage? Will the audience be able to appreciate it, even without having necessarily seen the ad?

REFLECT

Once you've gone through this full exercise once, you may find that you can read the subtext of ads much more quickly, even in real time, as you're watching. See if this happens. Watch the ads with more intention, more closely. What is *really* being sold? How are they selling it to you?

Do your newfound powers change the effect ads have on you?

What messages about our culture are being reinforced in these texts?

WRITING IS THINKING

The base unit of writing is not the sentence or the word; it is the idea.

The base unit of writing is the idea, because writing is a process of thinking.

Words and sentences only come into play as the material we use to express our ideas. Believing that sentences are primary would be like saying the key to good art is the paint in the tube. In the absence of the idea, there are no sentences to be made, just like the paint is useless unless an artist has sufficient inspiration.

If we consider writing as thinking, we see that all parts of the writing process are properly defined as writing, even if we are not actively putting words on the page. I am often writing when I'm walking the dogs or in the shower. When I am in the midst of a difficult project, I will sometimes wake up in the middle of the night and realize I've somehow been writing in my sleep.

Often the specifics of the sentence are the very last thing that takes shape. If you are struggling over a sentence to little avail, it may be that you're not done with the thinking yet. If that's the case, you can do what I do: put in a placeholder that says, SOMETHING LIKE THIS, BUT NOT SOUNDING SO DUMB.

Try to be a little nicer to yourself than I am to myself, though. Recognize that because writing is thinking, we have to be forgiving of ourselves when the right ideas don't arrive on a timely basis.

And of course the best words and the optimal sentences to express an idea depend significantly on the rhetorical occasion, particularly the audience. The same idea may be expressed in many different ways, each tailored to a different audience.

We should also recognize that because writing is thinking, the arrival of an idea may cause us to return to an earlier part of the writing process. An idea may occur that seems to need support from a secondary source, putting us back in research mode briefly before we return to drafting. We often write our way into new ideas, which may require a new draft as we realize the assumptions we started a draft with have changed.

When we are thinking at the top of our game, we are creating knowledge, something that did not exist before we brought it to life and that could only come into existence through a unique intelligence—the writer.

To me, this is the best part about writing, the feeling that at any given moment I may teach myself something I didn't know before. It's like finding a little bit of treasure squirreled away inside your own brain you didn't know was there until your persistence and dedicated thinking revealed it.

Sometimes this happens right after moments of great frustration, as the words seem to fail, but it was never a problem with the words. I just needed to unearth the idea.

It can be tempting to try to think through an entire piece of writing before starting to put words on the page, but this is a trap. The writing itself will always reveal something hidden.

You will know when you are writing, even if words aren't piling up, because you will be thinking.

What's So Funny?

(Rhetorical Analysis of a Work of Humor)

During the opening monologue of the 2015 Golden Globe Awards hosted by Tina Fey and Amy Poehler, Tina Fey delivered the following joke:

> George Clooney married Amal Alamuddin this year.
>
> Amal is a human rights lawyer who worked on the Enron case, was an adviser to Kofi Annan regarding Syria, and was selected to a three-person UN commission investigating rules of war violations in the Gaza Strip.
>
> So tonight her husband is getting a lifetime achievement award.

The in-person audience of Hollywood celebrities laughed, as did I. We got the joke.

But what is the joke? Why do we recognize it as funny? And, perhaps more interestingly, what comment does this kind of joke make about the broader culture we live in?

Writing for National Public Radio, Linda Holmes said of the Clooney joke, "It makes for a particularly pointed and effective reminder that the adulation afforded to actors is not based on merit, that the celebrating of their careers doesn't hold up to much scrutiny, and that a woman being glamorous and gorgeous and married to an actor doesn't make her, first and foremost, that" (https://www.npr.org/sections/monkeysee/2015/01/12/376718642 /what-those-george-clooney-jokes-know-about-red-carpet -culture).

It's funny because it's true. I may be reaching on this, but I also think the reverse fits: it's true because it's funny. When we laugh at this kind of joke, it's often because our brains reflexively recognize something as true we haven't necessarily specifically acknowledged or articulated before. It *is* true that we venerate celebrities out of proportion to their on-the-ground accomplishments. It is also true that women who marry famous men, no matter how accomplished they may be in their own right, are often reduced to what Linda Holmes calls a "red-carpet accessory."

We can uncover and understand a lot about a culture by critically examining the culture's artifacts—those things that are produced by the culture. Jokes are cultural artifacts.

In this experience, your job is to answer the questions, "What's so funny?" *and* "What does it say about us that we find this particular thing funny?" by looking closely at a single humorous text.

AUDIENCE

Your audience is a curious bunch of people who enjoy being shown aspects of the culture they may not have immediately grasped. Your goal is to have the audience exclaim, "I never would have thought of that," after reading your analysis.

They will not necessarily have experienced the text you're parsing, so you'll have to consider how to deal with that in your writing.

PROCESS

1. Find a humorous text.
You'll want to choose something neither too long nor too short. A single joke may not be sufficient, but an entire stand-up routine may be too long. A bit from a standup comedian or a single sketch from a show like *Saturday Night Live, Inside Amy Schumer,* or *Key & Peele* often works well. It could be a written text like a cartoon or piece from the *Onion* or *Reductress.* Meme jokes can work well too, as memes are definitely cultural artifacts.

Choose something you genuinely think is funny that you also suspect contains a cultural subtext that may be relevant to your audience. You don't need to grasp the subtext instantly. You just need to suspect it's present, waiting to be unearthed.

It's usually best to choose a text that is new to you, unless you're confident you can see the familiar with fresh eyes.

2. Process the text.
For this experience, I'm recommending the previously mentioned practice I'd one day like to develop a handier acronym for but that for the time being goes by ROAS. You have my permission to try to get away with using it in a moment of desperation in a game of Bananagrams, but it isn't actually a word.

React: First simply encounter the text as a living, breathing human being enjoying it. Once you've done this, record what happened. Where did you laugh? What kind of laugh was it? A rueful chuckle? All-out belly laugh? Something in between?

Observe: Look more closely at anything interesting you reacted to. What's going on? Look for details you might have missed the first time around or perhaps look at the specifics of how the humor was crafted or delivered. You also can now observe your own response more closely. What's happening to cause your laughter?

As you observe, ask questions of the text: Who would find it funny? What does the audience have to know to find it funny? Who gets it and who doesn't get it? Would anyone not find it funny, or even be offended?

Analyze: Start to shape some of the observations into a theory. In the example above, Linda Holmes has noticed a trend in jokes about George Clooney's marriage and extended that observation to a larger point about how women are treated in relation to famous men. She created insight and knowledge. Ultimately, for a fully realized piece of writing, you'll need more than one bit, but see what conclusions you can draw from your observations.

Synthesize: This is what will happen as you draft your piece. You'll work from those observations and bits of analysis, and hopefully have additional insights as you go. Think of it as a process of discovery in which what you have to say is revealed as you say it.

3. Write a discovery draft.

Working toward synthesis, start writing with the notion you may be surprised by what you find. Keep your audience in mind. Remember that they may not have experienced the text and may need some context to appreciate the observations and analysis that is to come.

For your audience (and yourself), think about how you're showing your reasoning on the page, how the analysis is built from your initial response and observations. If you share your findings without helping the audience appreciate how you got there, they may be less inclined to accept your analysis.

Remember your purpose: to reveal the cultural subtext and meaning of the humorous text. It's funny because it's true. What's the truth the text is telling?

4. Process your draft.

What have you done? Do you have a central idea? Often after a discovery draft, you may write your way into your main point, but it's a little buried. If you had to write an old-school 140-character tweet conveying the main idea of your essay, what would it be?

If you're having a hard time articulating your main idea, you may have what I call a "laundry list" draft, a bunch of individual items not yet unified. That's fine—better than fine, even. As you look at the list, can you make connections among the different items? Look for that synthesis.

At any time, feel free to go back to the text you're writing about and re-experience it, looking for fresh observations and analysis.

5. Revise.

This time around, as soon as you feel confident in your message, you'll really want to be thinking of your audience as you revise. You're walking them through an experience and subsequent analysis. Think of them being in the same state you were prior to all the thinking you've been doing about your text.

Try to anticipate any questions or confusion they may have and address it before, or just as, it arises.

6. Edit, polish.

When you're writing for real people, this stuff always matters. This is the kind of piece that makes for ready content for culturally engaged websites. Give your piece a good title that will intrigue the audience.

7. Title.

The text you've analyzed probably deserves mentioning in the title. If people are familiar with it or its subject or creator, you might have them intrigued enough to start reading.

REFLECT

E. B. White said, "Humor can be dissected, as a frog can, but the thing dies in the process and the innards are discouraging to any but the purely scientific mind."

Do you agree or disagree with the legendary children's book author and writer of other stuff? Is the text you wrote about no longer funny? If so, why? What has killed it?

Has something of value replaced the humor, or do you wish you'd just left it all alone?

If you disagree, what's E. B. White missing? What does he have wrong? Why does the funny stay funny?

REMIX

Find something you used to think was funny but are no longer amused by. What happened to change your response? For me, I'm thinking of Eddie Murphy's stand-up routines from the 1980s, when I was a young teenager. At the time, I had the bits practically memorized, but today I find many of the jokes offensive, misogynistic, and especially homophobic. I cringe when I watch what used to split my sides.

What changed? Lots of things. I got older and my own attitudes changed, but clearly the biggest change has been in public attitudes toward the kind of subjects Eddie Murphy mined for his humor.

There's something interesting in there I could explore in an open-ended piece of writing with no specific purpose other than to discover some fresh insight about this thing I noticed. See if there isn't something for you to notice about something that's no longer funny to you.

What's Going to Happen?

(Playing the Pundit)

If I come back in another life, I'd like to be either a golden retriever or a pundit.

It'd be great to be a golden retriever, because everyone loves a golden retriever, and even as dogs go, they seem exceptionally happy-go-lucky.

The great thing about being a pundit is that you get to make predictions that are consistently wrong, sometimes in significant ways. Politics and sports seem to have the highest tolerance for bad punditry, but you can find someone willing to predict the future on just about any subject you care to name.

For this experience, you are going to join their ranks and attempt to predict the future, though rather than plucking your prediction out of thin air, you're going to undergo a rigorous process of research and inductive reasoning.

Even if your prediction turns out to be wrong, no one will be able to accuse you of not being thoughtful about it.

AUDIENCE

Your audience is curious, engaged, knowledgeable about the world, but also looking to you to demonstrate thoughtfulness and expertise. They want their thinking challenged in order to help them more deeply consider the issue you've decided to weigh in on.

PROCESS

1. Identify the subject area.
If you're going to present yourself as an expert, it's best to start by surveying the landscape where you have existing expertise. This not need be academic or credentialed expertise. It could be rooted in a passion or hobby. List anything you know something about. In my case, that list would include things like education, contemporary writers and publishing, and the Chicago Blackhawks hockey team. I used to know more stuff, but as you age your areas of expertise tend to shrink in terms of number but increase in terms of depth.

2. Dig into the subject area.
Ultimately, you're looking to make a specific prediction concerning a single topic. This isn't a shotgun approach but an attempt to hit a bull's-eye with one shot. The initial prediction may be a gut-level guess, but your gut is likely to be more informed by reason and evidence than you know. Later you can go back and figure out where your gut instinct is coming from.

If I think about books and publishing, I realize that years ago when the Kindle first arrived and people were making predictions about digital reading ultimately taking over for printed books entirely, I was a skeptic. I believed (and still do) that the experience of reading on a screen is different from that of reading a physical book, and thus far I'm looking pretty prescient. Sales of physical books are actually going up a bit, while digital sales are relatively flat.

My biggest prediction and worry for education is that the increasing cost of tuition combined with declining public support for state institutions, community colleges, and universities will ultimately make the choice to pursue a college education an economically dubious proposition for those who aren't already wealthy enough (or fortunate enough) to pay without needing loans.

Either of these areas would be sufficient for me to move to the next step. You don't need to get locked into a single idea, even at this stage, and having different possible paths may pay off later if additional work reveals one path isn't as promising as you thought.

3. Research.

Your gut has told you one thing. Go looking around for evidence that either confirms or disproves your gut.

For my education topic, I could find data on the percentage of people going to college, the rate of tuition increase, how much college costs relative to other eras, the percentage of students who graduate with student-loan debt and the size of the average debt. I may find information that complicates my initial belief. For example, while it's true that college has become consistently more expensive and more and more students take on debt, as of this moment it appears to still be an economically sound decision provided you graduate.

At this stage, I'm trying to become as knowledgeable about my topic as possible. This often involves hopping from source to source, as one source will likely refer to others worth checking out.

You'll also want to be concerned if every source agrees with you. If you're having a hard time finding complicating information, change your search terms to approach the subject at a different angle.

4. Plan your case.

Here's where you consider your audience and their questions. They might care about some or all of the following:

What's going to happen?

Why do you say it's going to happen?

Who cares if it happens? Who is affected if it happens?

What are the big-picture implications if this prediction happens?

Should I be worried or excited, or some mix of both, about this happening?

Depending on your topic, the audience may care about other things as well. You should list any questions or concerns your audience may have.

5. Draft your prediction.

At some point, you should probably answer all of your audience's questions, but the order in which you answer them and how you go about answering them could vary widely. Read some works by others that contain predictions, to see how they start off, build their case, and then conclude.

For sure, you want to be conscious of providing evidence that will allow your audience to understand where you're coming from. Illustrating that evidence in a way that achieves maximum "information relevance" is advisable.

For example, one claim I would make about the increasing burden of college costs is that it is much more difficult to pay your way through college than ever before. When I was a student at the University of Illinois (1988–92), you could pay annual tuition with around five weeks of minimum-wage work in Illinois. As of 2017, paying a year's tuition at U of I would take approximately forty-eight weeks of minimum-wage work in Illinois.

By showing that tuition is not only more expensive but also more difficult to cover using routes that were previously possible,

I help give that particular evidence increased relevance. It's not just the numbers but what the numbers mean in a real-world context.

6. Test your prediction.
Have a test audience read your prediction, and then ask them, on a scale of one to ten—where one means they think what you've predicted is about as likely to happen as a cow sprouting wings and developing the ability to jump over the moon, and ten means if they could bet on what you've predicted, they'd put every last penny they own on it—how likely they think your prediction is to come true.

After that, you'll want to know which evidence they found most and least persuasive, as well as any evidence they thought was confusing or irrelevant.

Finally, ask if they have any questions you haven't answered that may be relevant to your prediction.

7. Revise, edit, polish, title.
As always, your credibility rests on the overall quality of your presentation.

REFLECT

How well did your gut reflect your final opinion about your prediction? If it was ultimately pretty true to the evidence, why do you think this was? If it was otherwise, what were you missing?

One of the weaknesses of punditry is the extent to which pundits rely on patterns of the past to predict the future. For sure, "history repeats itself" is a cliché because it holds some truth, but history doesn't repeat itself in identical ways, even when we see similar patterns. Good predictions require an ability to see when something has sufficiently deviated from previous patterns, creating a kind of new reality. Political and sports prognosticators are so often wrong because they almost exclusively try to fit the present to the past—this is how polling predictions work—but really good and exciting thinkers are able to see past the past, if you will.

How can you help yourself see past the past in areas where you're passionate and engaged?

REMIX

Take your big prediction, separate it from the evidence, throw it into the social media stream, and see what happens. How do people react? What can we learn about predictions and people based on how they react?

How persuasive is your prediction once stripped of its evidence?

WHY PROOFREADING IS SO DIFFICULT

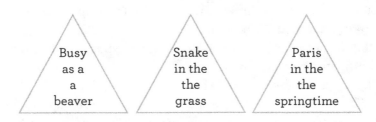

Busy
as a
a
beaver

Snake
in the
the
grass

Paris
in the
the
springtime

At first glance, one often doesn't see errors because the brain takes in the gist (especially with clichés) and thinks it saw "busy as a beaver" rather than "busy as a a beaver," because "busy as a a beaver" doesn't make any sense, so why would someone type such a thing?

This problem is related to a concept known as "perceptual set," which means what we expect to see sometimes influences what we actually see. This is especially true in reviewing our own writing because our brains know what we meant to say, so we often think we've said it, even though there may be a gap between our intentions and reality.

For example, the first time I typed the previous sentence I substituted "their" for "there." That error has nothing to do with my knowledge of proper word usage in the English language. I know when it's proper to use "their," "there," or "they're," but when I'm drafting, particularly when the ideas are flowing, my brain automatically defaults to "their."

Over time I've learned to double-check this particular tendency when I need to present a polished product. Becoming aware of the mistakes you often make can be helpful in improving your proofreading skills.

Here are some other recommendations for proofing and polishing your writing:

1. Know when it's time to start polishing.
While you're drafting and revising, it's sensible to fix any mistakes you can see, but the thinking required for creating ideas and the thinking required for polishing language are different. The first full draft of this manuscript I turn into my editor will be riddled with mistakes of grammar, syntax, even spelling, because I will still have much revising to do based on her feedback.

When building a house, you don't stop and sweep up the sawdust every time you cut a single board. It's a balance: you don't want the work site to be such a mess that you can't keep building, but nobody is going to move in while construction is under way.

2. Get help.

One of the best parts about having a publisher is that they employ professionals who are highly trained at copyediting and proofreading and whose job it is to flag my mistakes so I can correct them. I try to give the copyeditor as clean a product as possible, but they have experience and expertise I lack. The shame I feel when seeing all the errors caught by the copyeditor is deep but completely worth it.

But even nonexpert eyes can be helpful in finding the kinds of obvious errors we miss in our own work because of the problems of perceptual set.

3. Read your own work out loud to yourself.

This is an easy way to catch the kinds of errors that will irk the reader. It forces you to slow down and consider each word in ways that never happen when reading regularly, particularly when reading on a screen.

If you really want to get down to the sentence level, read what you've written from the bottom up, starting with the last sentence. This will completely short-circuit the part of your brain that is preoccupied with meaning and focus you at the sentence level. Only do this once you're really convinced your ideas and structure are in place.

4. Be aware of your limits and forgive yourself for your humanity.

Even with expert help, this book will be published with mistakes. I have yet to read a book that doesn't have any mistakes. It is immensely frustrating to open something you worked on so hard and find a mistake, but it is also inevitable.

This is not a free pass to turn in unpolished work because you can't expect perfection. One of the key skills and habits of mind in the writer's practice is recognizing the gap between "good enough" and "can't make it better." Paying attention to the proofreading and polishing part of the process is how this can be learned.

What If . . . ?

(Alternate History)

In 1984, one of the worst decisions in the history of making decisions occurred, altering the course of American, and perhaps even world, history.

In the 1984 NBA draft, with the second pick, the Portland Trail Blazers chose Sam Bowie of the University of Kentucky over Michael Jordan of the University of North Carolina.

Bowie, a seven-foot-one-inch center, was hobbled by injuries most of his career. He wound up playing a total of 511 games in the NBA, averaging 10.9 points and 7.5 rebounds per game, respectable numbers but not enough to keep him from being named the "biggest draft bust in history" by *Sports Illustrated* magazine.

Michael Jordan, as many know, became the greatest basketball player of all time. Six championships, five MVPs, and a starring role in *Space Jam*, in which he bands together with Bugs Bunny, Daffy Duck, and other *Looney Tunes* characters to defeat a band of animated Monstars, who have stolen the basketball ability of NBA stars like Charles Barkley, Patrick Ewing, and Muggsy Bogues.

As a lifelong Chicago Bulls fan, I am overjoyed by this accident of history, but it's worth asking: what if Michael Jordan had been a Portland Trail Blazer instead?

Questions of alternate history are fascinating exercises in research and reasoning. What would've happened if Al Gore won the 2000 election instead of George W. Bush? What if Adolf Hitler had stuck with art school or Harry Truman had decided not to drop atomic bombs on Japan? What if John Lennon wasn't murdered and the Beatles reunited? What if? What if? What if?

In the case of Michael Jordan and Sam Bowie, yours truly, as a Chicago Bulls fan for his entire life, would've spent many fewer hours enjoying the success of my favorite basketball team. I also never would've seen Michael Jordan enter a convenience store where I was waiting to pay for a Slurpee, grab a copy of a newspaper with his picture splashed on the cover of the sports page, flip a twenty on the counter, and stride back outside and into his Corvette.

Your task is to create an alternate history around the question "What would've happened?" by altering a single event in the past and then projecting events forward.

AUDIENCE

You audience is both interested in and generally knowledgeable about your topic. In the example above, my audience would be basketball fans, and they likely remember things like Sam Bowie being drafted before Michael Jordan or that Hakeem Olajuwon was the number one pick in 1984. Your audience is not made up of absolute experts—my audience doesn't know Michael Jordan's career stats off the tops of their heads—but they aren't blank slates, either.

You will need to remind them of some things, but they don't need massive dumps of information to engage with your analysis.

They're hoping to be provoked by your alternate-history theory. You are trying to persuade your audience that your invented past is plausible, but you should also expect them to challenge some of your claims. You are not spinning a fantasy. You're arguing from inferences and evidence. In the end, your goal is to make them believe such a past could've been at least possible had a single historical event been different.

PROCESS

1. Brainstorm possible topics.
Start with your interests, passions, and preoccupations. For obvious reasons, history is a promising area in which to find a good scenario for an alternate history, but as you can see from my example, it's not the only route. Even if you're not as knowledgeable as you wish, think of a topic you're really interested in so any research you do will be pleasurable for its own sake.

2. Pick a moment.
Pick a single chain in a past event and break it. Have the Trail Blazers draft Jordan. Have a young painter named Adolf Hitler be so praised for his work he winds up pursuing the life of an artist in Paris instead of becoming a genocidal maniac. Make sure the break is at least somewhat plausible. Remember that the event need not be big in and of itself. It just has to have ripple effects that change the path of history.

3. Research.
Research can take a lot of different forms, but it need not be formal or structured. The goal is to become knowledgeable about what happened and why it happened. The Portland Trail Blazers picked Sam Bowie because they thought they needed a center more than a guard like Jordan. This was a different era when a dominant seven-footer was thought necessary to compete for championships. "Fools, fools," I say, but that's hindsight talking. Understanding the context in which history happened is necessary to understanding the ways history could've been different.

4. Write the story.

What would've happened? Tell the reader. Remember the "story" part of "history."

5. Check your story.

Looking at your tale, what is the evidence you've included to support the likelihood of these events? How convincing is your evidence to the audience? Are there interpretations of the evidence other than what you've decided? Should you mention those possibilities in order to head off any audience objections to your theory? If history is a chain, are all of the links of events in your imagined history strong?

6. Revise, edit, polish, title.

The story is the main character of the piece, but you don't want any blemishes hindering engagement with the story. A title framed as a question that your piece answers is probably a good way to go.

REFLECT

This experience is a good opportunity to reflect on what you know now that you didn't prior to doing the writing. One of the most difficult parts about developing as a writer is the long, slow slog toward subject expertise.

You began with an area of interest and at least partial expertise, but you likely increased your subject expertise. For example, in drafting this experience I went digging around and found a quote from the general manager of the Portland Trail Blazers saying that they felt they already had a great shooting guard in a guy named Clyde

Drexler, who was awesome in his own right, having been named one of the fifty greatest players of all time in 1996. (I just looked that up right now: I know more than I did thirty seconds ago.)

If you pause to appreciate what you're learning, you may better appreciate how content knowledge translates into confidence with writing, and start to set a threshold for how much research you have to do to feel sufficiently comfortable to take on a topic.

This is also useful when you're midstream on a project, as you're more likely to recognize gaps in your knowledge that need filling.

REMIX

Let's switch to the realm of personal history. Can you think of any moments in your own life when a single choice or event may have altered its trajectory? For example, I first met my wife on a semi-blind date, filling in for someone who had been thrown in jail. I'm not sure we would have ever crossed paths otherwise. If that dude hadn't done whatever stupid thing put him in jail, I'd be living a markedly different life. It messes me up to even think about it sometimes.

What's a road not traveled in your own life? Explore your alternate personal history in a very different piece of writing.

PROCRASTINATION

When I ask a group of writers, regardless of age, experience, or accomplishment, how many of them are procrastinators, somewhere around 80 percent of them raise their hands.

My hand is raised.

There is something about writing that lends itself to procrastination. But in my experience as a writer and teacher of writing, procrastination comes in many different flavors.

Some procrastinate because they simply do not like writing and want to put it off as long as possible, the same way I will put off getting a flu shot. This dislike may be rooted in lack of confidence or lack of practice, but either way it's procrastination as avoidance of an unpleasant experience. In other words, they're afraid.

Some people are the opposite. They actually enjoy writing and are excited about the task but also recognize that doing the task means producing something that may not measure up to their own expectations, thus causing disappointment. In other words, they're afraid.

Some writers are paralyzed by the thought of having to show their writing to others, be it an audience, a teacher, or anyone else. In other words, they're afraid.

And believe it or not, others are not worried about their writing failing but are instead concerned that their work may be *too* successful. What if the next thing they write is the best thing they'll ever write and it's all downhill from there? Better to just not write at all. In other words, they're afraid.

Fear drives procrastination. Very rarely are these fears rational—though we may have a boss or teacher who has taught us to fear feedback—but just because they aren't rational doesn't mean they aren't real.

Most of the people who admit to procrastination also say that they rarely if ever fail to deliver on a deadline. This may mean pulling an all-nighter or sacrificing something they wanted to do, but the work gets done. The best cure for procrastination seems to be someone demanding we finish.

Except, in hindsight, most of us express regrets about the torture we put ourselves through having procrastinated. Why did I make it so hard on myself? I could have just started earlier. I was once given sixteen months to produce a book manuscript. I did it in the final four months, while also working full time, nearly driving myself to madness. I vowed to never do that to myself again.

Except, of course, I've done similar things to myself again and again.

The experiences in this book outline a detailed process from inception to completion in order to help mitigate procrastination. There's always some next step to take. But life rarely gives us these sorts of models. When this is the case, go back and reflect on how much of the writing process happens before words get on to the page and think about charting your own process to completion.

I wish I had a foolproof method for overcoming procrastination, but I do not. I struggle with it constantly. That said, some things can help.

First is to recognize the difference between normal procrastination, when you're not yet ready to put words on the page, and total avoidance, when you're pretending you don't actually have writing to do. Binging Netflix is not a part of the writing process, unless you're writing about *Orange Is the New Black*. Writing does not have to mean words accumulating on a page, but it does mean being engaged with some part of the writing process.

If words aren't coming, it may mean you're not done with the prewriting stage yet, and that's okay. You never know at what moment of the process the right idea is going to show up. Just be cautious that you're not avoiding the task entirely. It can be a tricky balance. Inspiration may strike while you're in the shower or cooking dinner, but it will only strike if you're directing at least some of your (possibly subconscious) attention to the task. If you're purely seeking distraction, it may be necessary to more explicitly reengage with the earlier prewriting.

Second is to get started with words on the page as soon as you have *anything* to say. For example, this chapter sat on my computer screen with only the title and first sentence for a solid week. I knew I wanted to write about procrastination, but I did not know what I wanted to say. By putting that title and sentence up, I'd at least started, dispelling a little bit of the fear.

A complete piece of writing is never going to arrive all at once. Get started, add bits as they come to you, and over time they will accrue into something meaningful. Think of it like pushing a boulder over a flat plain, trying to get it to a spot where it will roll downhill. At some point, your momentum will accelerate.

You may also want to try writing multiple things at one time. One cause of procrastination is the feeling that you have nothing to say, and the more you obsess about not having something to say, the harder it becomes to find something to say. This is a recipe for writer's block.

Writer's block is real. I know this because I've experienced it. In fact, I'm experiencing it as we speak. My cure for writer's block is to be juggling four or five projects at any given time.

I am always blocked on something. I'm never blocked on everything.

And often all I need to get unblocked is to truly let my mind take a rest from the subject. Sometimes a distraction will work, but often it's writing something else that will trigger reengagement with the things on which I was blocked.

The anticipation is almost always worse than the reality. We can really freak ourselves out when we're focused on worrying. When it comes to fighting procrastination, mostly I'm trying to do something to forget to be afraid.

How's It All Going to End?

(Judging the Apocalypse)

I first developed this assignment in a class where I had students read and study Cormac McCarthy's novel *The Road*. In the novel, a father and his young son travel through a postapocalyptic wasteland toward rumors of some semblance of a remaining civilization, but for the most part none of the markers of society we take for granted remain. The characters are concerned only with the barest necessities for survival.

In the novel, it's not clear how or why the world has collapsed, and the class enjoyed speculating about the possibilities. At some point in the discussion, a student asked me if I thought the world was going to end (by which the student meant civilization), and I said I thought most definitely.

Another student asked if I thought it might happen in my (or their) lifetimes, and what kind of odds I'd give on us experiencing something like what happens in *The Road* or any number of other postapocalyptic narratives, like *The Hunger Games* or *Mad Max* or *The Handmaid's Tale*. Without thinking, I said I honestly thought the odds were pretty good that we'd be done in by one thing or another, if not in my lifetime, in theirs.

Cheery! Who says class can't be fun?

In this experience, you will first make a binary choice. Do you believe (as I do) that civilization as we know it will end? Or are you hopeful that we're up to whatever challenges we may face in the future, that humankind will persist forever, potentially even if or when the earth becomes uninhabitable?

Once you've made your choice, you'll create an argument supporting your choice.

If we're doomed, why? And what is going to precipitate our downfall?

If you're hopeful, why? And how will humans be able to persist?

And how certain are you of your conclusions, no matter which side of the divide you fall on?

AUDIENCE

The audience is going to be curious, but they may not be wildly enthusiastic when it comes to reading and thinking about the end of the world. It's an interesting exercise in the abstract, but it also requires us to delve into some potentially scary territory. I never would've even thought of the assignment if my students hadn't goaded me into it, because I don't actually enjoy spending time contemplating the end of civilization.

But to think through these potential threats and how we might mitigate them is also a valuable service. You're doing the audience a favor, although they may not recognize or thank you for it.

Your choice of civilization-ending event will dictate your consideration of your audience's attitudes and knowledge. Some threats are often publicly discussed, while others might be a little more obscure. Some may raise thorny political or cultural dimensions, which may impact receptiveness to your argument. For some topics, audiences will possess a lot of mistaken information that you may have to undo.

At the least, your audience should leave your piece significantly more knowledgeable about the issues on which you choose to write, even if they don't necessarily end up agreeing with you.

Think through these issues and proceed accordingly.

PROCESS

1. *Choose your path.*

Will civilization end or will humankind persist? There's no right or wrong answer to this question on its face, so what you choose will often be a reflection of your own attitudes and worldview. I tend toward pessimism when it comes to considerations of human nature, so I can't help but think we're doomed.

Other people have faith in human ingenuity, and believe our big brains and survival instincts will make sure we persist as a species indefinitely.

Your path is up to you.

2. *Choose your scenario.*

Whether you believe we're doomed or we will persist, we for sure will face threats to our continuing existence. In fact, we face them this very moment.

End-of-civilization scenarios divide into two broad categories, anthropogenic (man-made), and non-anthropogenic (naturally occurring).

Non-anthropogenic threats include a catastrophic meteor strike, the death of the sun, alien invasion, volcanoes, earthquakes, tsunamis, and disruption of the Oort cloud. (Look it up.)

Anthropogenic threats are things like population overload, global warfare, environmental disaster, global warming, and artificial intelligence leading to robot takeover, like in *The Terminator.*

Disease, the "end of men" (collapsing birthrates as portrayed in *Children of Men* and *The Handmaid's Tale*), peak oil, nuclear war, EMP, terrorism, the Rapture—the list of different threats goes on and on.

There are plenty of resources available to study possible civilization-ending events. Be cautious, though. Some of these are going to come from conspiracy theorists and may be interesting reading but not necessarily reliable.

You may see multiple problems on the horizon, but you only have room to pick one possible scenario for analysis and discussion. You're going to explain either how it's going to end us or how we're going to overcome it.

3. Do any necessary additional research.

Choosing your scenario likely required a fair bit of research. Now is a chance to do any additional research you think is necessary before you get rolling on a draft. You'll probably need to keep researching throughout the process, so don't delay writing for too long. The writing itself will reveal holes in your argument that will need to be filled by research.

At this stage, you should have enough to get going but likely not enough to get to the end. That's normal and expected.

4. Analyze the audience needs.

What questions is your audience going to have about your topic? Off the top of my head, they might ask the following:

What is it?
How would it end civilization?
Wait, what do you mean by "end" and "civilization?"
   (Meaning, what's going to be left afterward?)
How likely is this scenario?

Is there anything we can do to prevent it? Is there anything we should be doing to prevent it?

I don't know what order those belong in, and I don't know that they're comprehensive, but they're the kind of questions you should be thinking about.

5. Write.
Write something. Maybe it's a draft. Maybe it's an outline. Maybe it's an illustration or diagram representing what may happen to something specific if your doomsday scenario comes to pass. How much land is inhabitable? What kind of work will people do? What will day-to-day life be like? Write something that helps you think more deeply about your topic and audience.

6. Put it together.
Create a cohesive work of analysis, argument, and discussion that explores the question at the center of this experience.

Do it in a way that engages your audience's questions and meets their needs. This may take a fair amount of trial and error. Keep the goal in mind and keep shaping until you have something you feel good about.

7. Test it.
What questions do you want to ask your audience to see if you're hitting the target? Develop them and test them.

8. Revise, edit, polish, title.
What did you learn from your test audience? Are you persuasive? Are you sure you don't tip over into conspiracy theory territory? Do you have the right amount of intrigue without leaving the audience so frightened they don't want to read the whole thing?

REFLECT

Are you a survivor? If the apocalypse comes, are you going to do everything you can to keep going? I'm the kind of person who, if there's word of a nuclear strike and I see a great, glowing light in the distance, you'll find me sprinting toward it, hoping to be vaporized into ash.

My wife, on the other hand, is a survivor. She'd be like the characters in *The Walking Dead* and charge into the zombie hoard with a knife in her teeth, swinging a baseball bat.

Where does your attitude come from? I think my mentality was shaped by a 1983 television movie called *The Day After*. It follows the lives of people in Kansas who have survived an initial nuclear strike by the Soviet Union. The movie is cheap and cheesy by contemporary standards, but it was watched by more than a hundred million people when it first aired. I was thirteen years old, the right age to fully understand the implications of the story but not old enough to process the movie rationally. It gave me nightmares for weeks. I remember firmly deciding I didn't want to live like that.

In a lot of ways, my attitude was shaped by a rather safe and privileged upbringing. My instinct for survival has never been tested. (Knock on wood.) Sometimes, I view my own attitudes as a kind of character flaw, an affront to what's supposed to be our basic biological drives. On the other hand, I really, really don't think I want to stick around for the really bad stuff.

But what about you? Imagine being confronted with living in the midst of your apocalypse. Would you keep fighting to stay alive no matter what? What are your attitudes rooted in?

REMIX

Write a narrative set in your scenario that reflects your argument. You have a setting and situation. Add character and plot, and you have everything you need.

RESEARCH AND ARGUMENT

We often think of an argument as something we're trying to win, even if that means bending or breaking the rules. If it's an interpersonal argument, sometimes we resort to making up stuff in order to claim a (usually temporary) victory. It seems more important to win than it is to be right. If an argument has a winner and loser, who wants to be the loser?

But arguments in writing or public discourse of any kind are conducted for the benefit of the audience. The goal is not to win but to make sure everyone leaves the argument knowing more about the subject than before being exposed to the argument.

Making this kind of argument a more common feature of everyday life would probably result in greatly improved public spaces where people are less angry on social media. If we were less concerned about being viewed as the winner, and more concerned about being truthful and accurate, a lot of the free-floating BS that makes its way through the culture would be a little less foul smelling.

When we think of arguments this way, even the "loser" of the argument gains, because they possess information and insight they lacked before. It can be difficult when you've been shown to be wrong, but that temporary difficulty makes it more likely you'll win the argument next time.

For example, we could ask a question like, "Is going to college a good thing?"

On average, definitely. People with college degrees tend to have better outcomes, and not just economically. They report a greater sense of overall well-being also.

But different people go to college for different reasons, and the costs of going to college can vary greatly. Over the last twenty-plus years, the cost of college tuition has increased significantly. More students than ever graduate with great amounts of debt. Those who attend some college but don't graduate often have difficulty paying back loans or other related debt. Even as more and more people choose to go to college, we've made the path to success far more costly. Because of this, college may not be a universal best choice.

Good argument can seek to illuminate this issue in a lot of different ways. Economists may look at the cost-benefit in monetary terms of different paths in postsecondary education. Sociologists can look at how and why students from different backgrounds may make different choices when it comes to going to college.

The experiences in this section are designed to develop the writer's practice in the context of having these kinds of arguments.

The first four experiences, "What Do They Mean?" (summary and response), "Huh? Say What?" (translation), "Why Should I Trust This?" (understanding sources), and "Hey, Whaddaya Know?" (trivia questions and annotated bibliography) are focused on some of the fundamental skills and attitudes that make it easier to write effective arguments.

Essentially, in order to argue effectively we need to be able to present all aspects of someone else's argument and understand where their argument comes from and evaluate the building blocks on which their argument rests.

We also need to be able to handle sources by locating and digesting them, and utilizing one of our most important habits of mind, curiosity, to follow a trail of information in order to make sure we've accessed the best, most accurate stuff.

After that, you'll be arguing, starting with an "impossible" argument before moving on to other varieties of argument, each of which originates in something you believe to be important.

For these sorts of experiences, revision may work a little differently than it has in the previous pieces. Sometimes, when making an argument, we'll get to the end of a draft and realize, for whatever reason, it just didn't fly. It may be that we were mistaken about the strength of the evidence or that a claim we rested our argument on is weaker than we figured, or that the draft revealed we need to target a different audience. The list of reasons why a draft may go wrong are endless.

When this happens, for revision, it's usually best to start a fresh draft, with a blank page, rather than trying to work with the existing text. This doesn't mean the original draft was a waste. In fact, it's the opposite. The draft allowed you to do the thinking necessary to find the right approach.

Writing and revision often works this way. When there are more moving parts in a particular experience, revision can become a more involved process. Don't fear it.

Consider each argument as a chance to exercise your own thinking and reasoning abilities. Even if the end result isn't as great as you'd wish, the exercise was worth doing and will help lead to better results in the future.

What Do They Mean?

(Argument Summary and Response)

One of the fundamental skills in making arguments is to be able to accurately convey the arguments of others. In writing teacher circles, we often call this "summary," but I've found that this word can be somewhat misleading. A good summary doesn't just repeat what someone else said as a kind of regurgitation of content; it distills the original text down to its core meaning.

A good summary zeroes in on the main idea of the text, the author's point. It captures the forest without describing all the individual trees. When you summarize, it is as though you are standing in the shoes of the original author and are the vessel through which their ideas flow. Now, when you write something that brings a summary of another person's argument together with your own argument, you may reveal strong disagreements (or agreements, or a mix of both) with this other person's argument, but while summarizing the other's argument you're trying to be as true to the original as possible.

Ideally for the audience, the summary stands in the place of having to read the original text. They can trust you, the summarizer, to accurately convey what this other person was claiming to be true.

For a summary to be effective, it must be shorter, often a good deal shorter, than the original article; otherwise, why are your summarizing it?

AUDIENCE

The audience is curious about an argument put forward in the article you're summarizing, but they don't have time to read it. They've come to you to find out what the fuss is about. They trust you and won't be immediately checking on the accuracy of your summary, but they will obviously have enough information to do so, if they desire, at some future point.

If they find out you've steered them wrong, you may permanently lose credibility as a source to be trusted.

PROCESS

1. Find an article with an argument.
These are readily available. Every newspaper has an op-ed (opinion and editorial) section. Websites are constantly publishing arguments, which is why we can spend so much time arguing with total strangers on social media. Make sure the article comes from a verifiably credible source, and choose an argument in which you're interested.

2. Read the article.
Read the article once through to get the gist. With practice, you can usually do a mostly accurate summary after a single read-through, but it's a good habit to do one read, then go back and check your understanding.

Are there any parts you kind of get but not entirely? What about vocabulary that you mostly understand in context but are also maybe guessing about a little bit?

Perhaps the article refers to an incident or idea in a way that assumes you're familiar with it, but you aren't. Take some time to fill any gaps in your knowledge, until you feel you have an excellent handle on the article. These days, we have wonderfully handy tools at our fingertips (or thumb tips) to work with.

3. Draft a summary.

Keeping your audience and purpose in mind, draft your summary. You'll want to focus on the argument, really distill it to its essence. As you write, you should give the argument to the author, using their name and a verb that conveys the fact that they're the one making the argument, such as: "Warner believes writing an accurate summary is a 'fundamental' skill for writing arguments."

Notice the difference between that sentence and something like this: "Warner wrote about how summaries are used in arguments."

The second example doesn't share any claim I (Warner) made. It describes content rather than summarizes argument. Verbs like "believes," "claims," "argues," even "says" (provided it's followed by a claim) help make sure you're focusing on the original author's argument.

Once you've identified the main idea, think about your audience. After hearing the central claim, they're likely to be thinking, "Why? Why does this person believe this thing I'm being told?"

Use the remainder of the summary to tell them why the original author believes what they believe. You will be supporting that initial claim about the main argument with a series of other claims. It's like those Russian nesting dolls. You start with the big doll by making a claim, open it up, and then each doll is another claim that supports the one before it.

4. Test the summary.

Find someone who has not read the article you're summarizing and have them read your summary.

When they're done, without letting them refer to your summary, see if they can accurately summarize your summary.

Next, have them read the original article. Have them write a one-sentence summary of the main point after reading the article. Does it match up with what they got from your summary?

If something is off, discuss it with your tester. What meaning are they getting that you're missing? It's possible they're off base and you're on target. Hash it out until you're satisfied that you've accurately captured the original.

5. Revise, edit, and title.

A summary rarely stands by itself, but it's worth taking the time to address any of your reader's questions or concerns.

REFLECT

This is going to sound odd, but I believe reading is one of our most difficult skills. It sounds odd because everyone we're talking about here knows how to read, but it is very hard to read well, and there are a lot of forces working against allowing us to read for deep understanding and engagement.

When a reading is forced on you, sometimes it can feel overwhelming, making skimming highly tempting. Sometimes the reading seems initially dull or uninteresting, either dividing our attention or leading to the old "I ran my eyes over the words, but I don't remember a thing" sensation I know so well.

Often we're incentivized to read quickly, gleaning the gist because the gist might be enough to figure out a question on a multiple-choice exam or convince someone we laid eyes on the document, but in the process we often miss something. When writing a summary, this can turn into a game of telephone, where a message is passed around the circle. As the original message moves from person to person, each person misses a little bit in turn, and the meaning ultimately becomes distorted in large, not small, ways.

I know I experience this in my own writing, but it's true when I read student work as well. I'm so conditioned to look for mistakes that I start to see flaws where they aren't present, or I may overlook virtues because I'm too busy focusing on other things.

Reading deliberately, checking my understanding, and not settling for the gist has become a really important skill for me. I don't always employ it, and it's not always necessary, but I know when I need it, it's there.

After this experience, maybe try practicing being more deliberate in your reading. When the reading is important, I think you'll find it actually saves time. When you need to make use of what you've been reading, you'll have a much better handle on what you've read.

REMIX

Once you've crafted a good summary, it's time to respond with an argument of your own.

Do you agree or disagree with the original author's opinion? Or is it some mix of the two? On the one hand, I believe X, but on the other hand, I believe Y.

A response to an original summary seeks to extend the argument by adding to it. This is not just a chance to say someone else is wrong (or right). It's a chance to extend the conversation.

The best way to think of it is to go back to your audience. Think of them as an interested third party who is trying their best to understand the issue being argued over. Your response is meant to enhance their understanding.

Make sure you start your response by declaring where you stand (agree, disagree, or a bit of both), followed by answering the likely next question, "Why?"

Focus on satisfying the audience's curiosity over this issue while also trying to be the most persuasive voice in the chain of argument. This means not only being clear with your own claims but offering evidence and argument in support of those claims.

Huh? Say What?

(Research Translation)

Just about every day in the news you'll hear or read something like "Based in research coming out of [very important and impressive sounding place] . . ." Because a news reader or news publication is presenting this research that has come from this impressive place, we're inclined to trust it, but should we?

I find academic research intimidating to read, even having been exposed to it for more than twenty years. And yet when I see reporting on research I'm familiar with, I often find mistakes, overgeneralizations, misinterpretations, exaggerations. It's frustrating when I know something is off. It also makes me wonder if something is off more often than I know when I hear about research in areas I'm not familiar with.

Academic research may embrace jargon that seems obscure to the layperson. The procedures make my head spin, and the statistical findings, with their confidence intervals and standard deviations, are equally confounding.

It's important to remember that academic research is written for specific audiences and with specific purposes in mind. All the stuff that seems confusing to a layperson helps other academics judge the underlying rigor with which the authors approached their research. Using jargon or terminology that seems obscure to me but is common in the specific field signals belonging to that field—that the author(s) is a member of the particular tribe for whom this research is conducted and is of interest.

This doesn't necessarily make academic research elitist or exclusive. If you sat down in the office of a coaching staff for a professional sport, you'd be equally subject to jargon or terms that seem foreign and confusing. It's a way for people within a culture to speak to one another.

There are some writers who specialize in "popularizing" academic research. Malcolm Gladwell, a writer for the *New Yorker*, is perhaps the most well known, though many academics are critical of the way he sometimes ignores the complexities of the research he popularizes.

But the vast majority of published research never breaks out of the academic world. This experience is designed to achieve two things: (1) get you working with academic research in order to up your comfort level with texts that are often complex and foreign, and (2) do a favor for the academics who publish their research by "translating" their findings for a more general audience.

This will also be an excellent challenge to your reading skills, since it may initially feel like diving into a foreign language.

AUDIENCE

Your audience consists of regular people who are curious and like to learn new things about the world but probably don't make a regular habit of perusing publications such as the *Journal of Supply Chain Management* or the *Journal of Biosensors and Bioelectronics* or the *Journal for Maritime Research* or the *Journal of Literary Semantics*.

(All of these exist for real.)

They want to know what the researchers have found in their

research, but they don't want to do the hard work of reading and interpreting the academic research for themselves.

You goal is to wow them by telling them something cool they didn't already know. It need not be life changing or earth shattering, but you're aiming for something they might want to pass along to someone else, like that trees and plants can apparently communicate with each other through a network of underground fungi, as found in the research of Suzanne Simard of the University of British Columbia.

That's cool, right?

You'll want to provide a sufficient translation of the original academic research to give your audience enough information to pass on the cool idea to someone else.

PROCESS

1. Choose the journal and article.
You can easily find lists of academic journals online at Wikipedia and elsewhere. If you have access to an academic library, you will find the available resources through the library's online interfaces for journals.

My recommendation is to start with a subject area of interest and then look for journals under that subject. When you find an interesting-looking journal, start browsing individual articles. The article abstracts should give a good indication as to whether a more thorough look at the entire article is warranted. You only need one article, and as long as there's an interesting takeaway in the findings it'll work for our purposes.

2. Digest the article.
Notice I did not say "read" your article. Sure, you'll read it, but this kind of text often requires a process that focuses on what you need

to meet your objective, rather than digging into every last morsel of information. Remember your purpose and audience. You'll want to read the whole article, but there will be much information that will be largely irrelevant to your goals. For example, the specifics of a research sample are important for researchers who may want to try to replicate the research, but you may just need to know that the sample was random or a sample of convenience. You're more interested in why this sample was used than in the particular nitty-gritty.

For the most part, you'll want to concentrate on the findings and implications (sometimes also called "discussion"), which is where the results of the research and why the research is important is shared. Make sure you have a deep understanding of this material. This may require additional reading in sources other than the article. If there is a term or idea you don't understand, seek outside resources that will help you understand it.

This is what is meant by "digesting" the article. You're not going to be able to bluff your understanding.

3. Translate the article.
Keeping your focus on your audience's needs, attitudes, and knowledge, tell them what's up with the research. Think about how to hook their interest and then satisfy their questions and curiosity once their interest is hooked.

For example, if I said, "Did you know that trees can talk to each other?" you'd say something like, "Whatchoo talking about?" My next sentence would add depth and clarity to my initial statement. Once I'm done with that, my audience likely has another question they want answered, maybe something like, "Who would study such a thing?" or "Why should I believe you?," in which case I'd likely go deeper into who conducted the research, how it was conducted, and why forestry scientists are interested in researching these questions.

4. Test your translation.

Find an audience and have them read your translation. Ask them to rate their interest in repeating your message to someone else on a scale of one to ten where one means, "I'd like to actively forget I even read this thing," and ten means, "I have to go find a tall building and a megaphone so I can shout this fascinating information to the world."

After that, ask them to repeat what they believe they've learned. If they're going to be broadcasting the message to the world, you want to make sure the message is accurate.

5. Revise, edit, polish, title.

Utilizing your audience feedback, as well as your own reflections on your draft and how well it engages your audience and purpose, revise your translation accordingly.

A title that captures the most interesting nugget of the research will help hook the audience.

REFLECT

How long did it take you to digest the article? Do you feel more confident in your ability to interact with this kind of specialized research and writing? If so, what technique or skill you employed will be most useful going forward?

If not, what do you think you need to work on in the future to increase your confidence?

REMIX

For fun, do a reverse translation: take something nonacademic and write it in a highly authoritative style and tone. What are the traits of the expert voice you are trying to mimic?

THE PERILS OF "OBJECTIVITY"

One of the most corrosive beliefs I find among developing writers is the idea that in their writing, they should strive for objectivity.

I think there are a lot of reasons for this. For the past thirty or so years, schools have been focused on assessment and standardization. Students are asked to identify a single "correct" answer. When applied to writing, this suggests there is an objective standard by which writing is to be judged.

There isn't.

Another reason is that some people like to claim a kind of rhetorical high ground by declaring themselves to be purely rational, as though they've achieved a kind of Spock-like view of the world. Those who do this are, of course, kidding themselves, unless they are actually Mr. Spock, who is a fictional character.

Some researchers may imagine their work to be objective, and in some hard sciences objective observation is the modus operandi, but all research is inherently subjective, starting with the choice of what to research. Those who get away with claiming they are objective where others are not are more likely simply working in a kind of default mode that has not yet been examined for its biases.

In writing, there is no virtue to objectivity, partly because it's impossible to achieve, and partly because no one really wants to read objective writing. The idea that a writer should spend their time trying to achieve objectivity in their expression is a colossal waste of everyone's time.

This doesn't mean anything goes, however. In fact, the writer's responsibilities are far deeper and more important than projecting an illusion of objectivity.

As you write, you should be less concerned with objectivity and more focused on discovery. If you learn something you didn't know before you started writing a piece, you're on the right track. It's a heck of a lot more fun too.

Consider something like a movie review. By definition, a movie review must be opinionated, not objective, because there is no objective standard for what makes a good movie. Even the crappiest movies get some positive reviews.

Instead of objectivity, we should embrace other values, things like transparency, fairness, accuracy, and openness. If you're doing a review and it stars a performer whose very existence puts your teeth on edge, you do not need to pretend this is not the case. In fact, pretending it's not the case and hiding this fact from the audience is a great disservice.

Instead, you should be transparent, declaring your bias to the audience up front, so they can evaluate your opinion in the light of your bias.

Rather than striving for objectivity, the goal is to develop a critical sensibility, a way of seeing the world that allows you to evaluate the claims and beliefs of others and weigh them against your own beliefs. Strong writing comes from strong beliefs well expressed.

At the same time, we should be open to changing our beliefs should experiences and information warrant. This is where openness comes in to play.

Our values, on the other hand, are relatively immutable, unlikely to shift. Often our beliefs change when we realize an existing belief is in conflict with our underlying values.

If you are striving to be accurate, fair, truthful, and transparent, you are fulfilling your responsibilities to the audience. Claiming objectivity is a lie, and we definitely try not to lie to our audiences.

Why Should I Trust This?

(Understanding Sources)

In a study conducted between January and June 2016, researchers at Stanford University tested the "civic online reasoning ability" of more than 7,800 middle school and high school students across twelve states.

The study defined "civic online reasoning" as "The ability to evaluate digital content and reach warranted conclusions about social and political issues: (1) identifying who's behind the information presented, (2) evaluating the evidence presented, and (3) investigating what other sources say" (http://www.aft.org/ae/fall2017/mcgrew_ortega_breakstone_wineburg).

The Stanford researchers found the results "disturbing."

Essentially, they found these middle school and high school students to be easily fooled by misinformation. In one task, fewer than 10 percent of those tested were able to identify a website presenting itself as a neutral source on minimum-wage laws and regulations as what was in reality the product of a partisan group linked to the US restaurant industry.

These findings are not surprising, and the difficulty of navigating the flood of content on the Internet is not limited to middle school and high school students. Much of the information we encounter on the Internet presents itself as true without offering any obvious way to judge its veracity. Factor in the influence of "confirmation bias," our willingness to accept something as true as long as it aligns with our existing beliefs, and we have an online atmosphere that makes it very difficult to discern what is true and what is not.

It is important to be able to make these distinctions, because, in the words of the Stanford researchers, "Credible information is to civic engagement what clean air and water are to public health."

Determining the accuracy and trustworthiness of online information benefits from a process called "lateral reading," which involves leaving the source you're trying to assess.

This experience has two purposes:

1. To practice a process for checking online information for accuracy.

2. To spread the word to others about *how* to do this, by describing the process you used to determine whether a particular fact or source was reliable or unreliable.

AUDIENCE

Imagine someone has come to you with a source or fact, and they're not sure if it's true or not. They've asked you for help in determining its accuracy but also in better understanding *why* they should trust or not trust the information. Your piece should leave the audience better armed to engage in their own online fact-checking process having learned from your example.

PROCESS

1. Find a source you want to check.
Potentially dubious sources are pretty easy to locate. They frequently circulate on social media. A good way to potentially

identify one is to be alert to a moment when your own confirmation bias may have kicked in: when you see information you desperately want to be true, but that desire is so intense, it may be overriding the rational part of your brain.

2. *Examine the questionable claim.*

Rather than examining the source itself for clues to its validity, use the tools of the Internet to find out as much as you can about the claim and the source.

Mike Caulfield, a professor and director of blended and networked learning at Washington State University Vancouver, recommends a three-step process (http://hapgood.us/2017/03/04/how-news-literacy -gets-the-web-wrong):

1. Check for previous fact-checking work

2. Go upstream from the source

3. Read laterally

The quickest way to check on a questionable claim is to see if someone else had a similar suspicion and if they've already studied the issue. A quick web search asking if something you're not sure about is true may lead you to a fact-checking website that discusses the claim and the evidence. While this may not be sufficient to satisfy the whole question, you're in the midst of an ongoing discussion about the claim rather than isolated, trying to assess the claim only by looking at the original source.

By going "upstream," Caulfield means tracing the claim to its original source. If we can find the original source, we stand a better chance of understanding the origins of the claim.

For example, you may have heard a factoid floating around saying something like 65 percent of children will work in jobs that don't yet exist. Benjamin Doxtdator, a teacher and education researcher, got curious about the origin of this claim, questioning its validity. After examining dozens of sources that made that claim or something similar, he found that the original idea of children stepping into a world of jobs that don't yet exist dates at least to the 1960s. The 65 percent figure is frequently cited as being from a source that doesn't actually contain that claim.

This is a factoid that circulates like an urban legend, sounding true enough that people don't question it (http://www.longviewon education.org/field-guide-jobs-dont-exist-yet).

But they should. Good writers question everything.

"Read laterally" means reading what other people say about the source of the claim. With the proliferation of digital media, it can be difficult to stay on top of every last source of information and be aware of any potential biases. Some sites are even specifically designed to be deceptive. Learn what you can about the site and the author making the claim in order to help assess the credibility. If you have a hard time finding lateral information about a source or author, that may tell you something important.

Ultimately, you're looking to surround the claim and be able to convey as much background about it as possible for the benefit of your audience. If the claim turns out to be true, you'll want to be convincing as to why it's true. If it's not true, you may need to tell your audience what is true.

3. Plan your case.

Your job is to report your findings. This involves informing your audience as to what you set out to do, and then walking them through what you did, and finishing with your conclusions. You will obviously be making claims of your own about the information you're checking, so you want to be very careful about tracking your own process. At every turn, the audience will be asking, "How do you know that?" Once you have answers ready for every time they will be tempted to ask this question, you're ready to report.

4. Write your report.
Write a report that meets your audience's needs while attending to their attitudes and knowledge. The attitudes and knowledge may be especially important. In an era when long-standing mainstream journalistic outlets are sometimes criticized as "fake news," you may need to go as far as to explain why—even though they sometimes make mistakes—we believe these institutions to be trustworthy.

5. Test your report.
Give your report to an audience that may be unsure about the truth of the claim you're checking. If they're not already familiar with the claim, show (or explain) it to them before giving them your report.

Are they convinced by your report? If so, ask them what they found most persuasive. If not, what else do they need to know?

6. Revise, edit, polish report.
Revise your work until your audience finds it convincing.

Edit and polish it in case you have future need for it. If you believe you've done a good job, it may be worth putting it on the Internet so others who run across the same questionable information can benefit from your hard work.

REFLECT

Imagine you run across something you suspect is dubious, but you don't have the benefit of outside research to compile a convincing case. What could you do to convince an audience that the dubious claim is untrue or at least sufficiently questionable that they shouldn't be so quick to circulate it further?

For example, in early April of 2018 I was delighted to see in the Twitter feed for the Kruger National Park in South Africa a picture of an African elephant cradling a lion cub in its trunk, with the mother lion walking alongside. The caption said that to help the lion, the elephant carried the cub for three kilometers.

How cute! I thought. When my wife got home, I eagerly told her about it, this amazing sight at a game reserve in South Africa. My wife, a veterinarian deeply knowledgeable about all things animal, declared such a thing impossible. "They're natural enemies."

I dug through my Twitter feed for the picture, ready to prove her wrong. Just as I was about to triumphantly produce the photo, I noticed the exact date on the tweet: April 1, 2018.

The post was a hoax put out by the park. Looking more closely, I could see it wasn't even a particularly good Photoshop job, but I had been fooled because part of me wanted to believe that real-life wild animals could enact something out of *The Lion King*.

As another example, take that factoid about 65 percent of the jobs today's children will one day hold not yet existing. Could you at least create doubt among those who believe that this is so true it's not worth questioning? How much have jobs changed? What jobs are new today that didn't exist twenty years ago? Have jobs with the same title changed so much that even though the name is the same, the job itself has changed? Does that count?

Practicing the kind of web literacy Mike Caulfield champions is vital to navigating today's information economy, but I also believe embracing an inherently more critical stance toward the information we encounter will allow us to keep from being so easily fooled.

Reflect on this experience. Can you think of anything—like me with the lion cub and elephant—that you now suspect might not be true?

REMIX

I have put two deliberate errors of fact into the introduction to this experience. Neither alters any important meaning, but they're inaccuracies nonetheless. Who knows, there may be unintentional errors as well. My desire is to make everything in this book as accurate as possible, but mistakes can still happen. Can you find and correct them? If you Tweet them to me @biblioracle, I'll respond to tell you if you're correct.

Hey, Whaddaya Know?

(Trivia Questions and

Annotated Bibliography)

Research = not much fun.

Learning stuff other people don't know so you can lord it over them = good times.

It is hard to say whether I enjoy trivia because my head is so full of it or because my head is full of it, I enjoy trivia, but either way I am one of those annoying people who will start a sentence with "Did you know . . . ?" and then tell you something you probably didn't know and don't care that you didn't know.

I also shout answers out loud at the television during *Jeopardy!* In my humble opinion, I would win approximately 80 percent of all *Jeopardy!* games if I could overcome my paralyzing fear of being on television, and as long as I could stay away from any geography-related category.

Research of one kind or another is a dominant aspect of my work as a writer, and the only way I became even half-good at it was to do it relentlessly, while also being allowed to research within areas of interest. It is truly difficult, if not impossible, to become a fully capable writer without possessing some solid research skills.

This is a way to practice research skills without getting too bogged down in the researchy part of research.

Your task is to write five trivia-ready questions about a single subject. But there's a twist: these trivia questions must not be answerable by searching a single Wikipedia page or on the first two pages of a Google search.

Each question and answer must include a citation—that is, a source (or sources) that proves their accuracy and truth. You may only use a source once. Five questions, five different sources.

PROCESS

1. Choose a subject area.

You'll want to head toward a subject you're already somewhat knowledgeable about, but you're also unlikely to think of a good question off the top of your head by mining your knowledge. You want enough familiarity to be able to interact with the sources where you will find your trivia and not scratch your head in confusion, but you don't need to be an absolute expert. You'll also want to think about narrowing down to a workable category. Sports or music or chemistry might be too broad, but 1990s NBA or early 2000s rap or fluorocarbons could work. You could go even narrower, like a single figure within your category: Michael Jordan or Kanye. Or even narrower, like a single game or album. Also be prepared to jump subject areas. You may begin researching and find more promising territory. Don't worry about that. You're searching for trivia gold. If one spot is dry, you move along.

2. Go searching.

You may want to start with the Internet, but in this case it's primarily a tool that will point you toward primary sources from which you can find interesting stuff that won't be readily available on the

Internet. You're not looking for trivia questions. You're looking to learn stuff. Take notes. Copy down sources. Be indiscriminate. Have you ever seen that game where they stick someone in a phone booth with a fan in the bottom and stuff it full of money and then turn on the fan, sending the money whirling around the booth? They always put like five thousand one-dollar bills and five one-thousand-dollar bills in the booth and you get to keep whatever money you can shove inside your clothes in sixty seconds.

The not-smart players grab bills one at a time, inspecting each one, trying to find the high dollar bills. The really not-smart ones then discard the one-dollar bills, sending them swirling back into the air, and possibly grabbing the same bill over and over. The smart players shovel as much money down their shirts, pants, socks, ears, and mouths as they can manage, hoping the high dollar bills are in there but settling for having as many one-dollar bills as possible.

Another way of saying this is don't judge, just gather as many sources from which to draw trivia as possible.

3. Digest the sources.

Read your sources, but not too closely. You're reviewing, skimming even, getting the gist so you know what your sources are about, where they might be useful for thinking about finding trivia. You're gleaning enough so if you decide to use them later, you'll know what they're useful for and can dive into them in more detail.

4. Catalog the most useful sources.

Take the five best sources (or more, if you think you have a lot of useful stuff) and write short summaries of what the sources contain, as well as any ideas you have for possible questions that may come from the sources. Remember that to get five good questions you might need to start with a much larger universe of possible questions.

5. *List all the stuff you now know that you didn't know before.*
Seriously, now that you've digested your sources, make a list of facts, figures, bits, and bites—you know, trivia.

6. *Write trivia questions.*
A good question is answerable but not by everybody. Of course you know the answer. When it comes to your subject, you know the answers because you've become a "Did you know?" person on your subject. You can write your questions in any form you wish: single answer, multiple choice, fill in the blank—whatever works best.

Sometimes you'll want to combine bits of trivia into a single question like, "These two songs, both with 'love' in the title, were number one on the charts back in . . ." Think about how you can invent a question based on the deep knowledge you have about what you've been researching.

7. *Test your trivia questions.*
Find people who might be good candidates for your questions and see how they do. Reward them if they get four or five out of five correct. People love that. If everyone is getting them all correct, your questions are too easy. If no one can get them, they're too hard. Try the questions on at least ten different people to see how they do.

8. *Revise the trivia questions to your satisfaction.*
You should aim for a spot where the average person gets three out of five questions correct. Some will get more. Others will get less. If your questions are too hard, rewrite them to make them easier

by going with multiple choice. Or look at how *Jeopardy!* sometimes gives contextual clues inside the questions themselves, so even if you don't know the answer, you can figure it out. Trivia that's too hard is no fun. Make it just right. You may even have to junk a question and try something different. Such is life.

REFLECT

Go back to step 4 of the process and look at that document. If done well, it likely resembles something academics call an "annotated bibliography." Annotated bibliographies are often assigned by writing teachers like me because we know they are very useful tools as part of the process of creating a researched piece of writing. Unfortunately, until you have done an annotated bibliography, it is hard to see how it might be useful, so when I assign them, students tend to view them as an arbitrary hoop to jump through in order to please the teacher, rather than as the way to help them process lots of information and become conversant on a subject relatively quickly.

Notice that you haven't read everything you've found, but you've also sort of read everything you've found. You have a sense of the kind of information that's out there about a subject, so if you were to write about that subject and ideas are forming and you realize you need a little bit of information, you know where to go looking.

Even though they seem like a lot of work, annotated bibliographies are real time-savers. They're also "living" documents that you can continually add to and update over time. They're a way of cataloging your own growing expertise.

We encounter so much information these days that it can be useful to have a tool to digest it more thoroughly, so if we need it later we don't have to start from scratch. We can go to our personal annotated bibliographies and review what we already "know."

For more formal and detailed information on annotated bibliographies in academia, do a search for "Purdue Online Writing Lab annotated bibliography."

REMIX

Now that you know all this stuff, what could you write from it? Form and purpose don't matter—meaning, I don't care, you pick. Think about the rhetorical situation—audience, purpose, message— and define and execute a writing experience for yourself.

Is a Hot Dog a Sandwich?

(Impossible Argument)

Problem: Some arguments are impossible to solve; i.e., no single answer will be satisfactory to everyone because the truth is likely somewhere in the middle.

This may be true of all arguments, now that I think about it, but let's not think about those other arguments for now. Let's think about an impossible argument.

Is a hot dog a sandwich?

Yes, absolutely? No, of course not? I bet you already feel passionately one way or another about this pressing issue and think those who differ are horribly misguided.

Good, let's argue.

Convince the audience your position on the question of whether a hot dog's a sandwich is correct. You must do this without relying on any outside research or additional sources. You will do it entirely based on your own experience and knowledge.

AUDIENCE

You are making your case to people who are interested and invested in this question, so pretty much anyone.

PURPOSE

The idea is to be persuasive. You want the audience to walk away agreeing with you. At the same time, exposure to the argument should leave your audience more knowledgeable about the subject than they were previously, even if they end up disagreeing with you.

PROCESS

1. What is a sandwich?

If you're going to argue about whether a hot dog is a sandwich, you might first need to define what makes a sandwich a sandwich. Spend some time figuring this out based on your own understanding of sandwiches.

2. Is a hot dog a sandwich?

Now decide where you stand. You've defined a sandwich. Does a hot dog fit the criteria?

3. Argue the opposite.

What is the best argument *against* your position? Take your arguments for your position and imagine someone saying, "Yeah, but . . ." What do you say in response to their "Yeah, but . . ."?

4. Write your argument.

Draft, revise, and edit a persuasive argument where you come down definitively on one side of this issue. Remember, no sources allowed.

REFLECT

Try the argument again, only this time you're allowed to use out-side sources to bolster your case. Where will you go for information? Why? What effect do you think these particular sources will have on your audience? What will be persuasive and why?

How much more effective is the argument when you use these sources?

Did any of the sources alter your opinion? Are you tempted to switch sides in the debate based on your review of the sources?

REMIX

See if you can come up with your own "impossible argument." What's something people could argue about endlessly that would be interesting and where the argument itself may help them to better understand the subject being argued over?

Hint: arguments about whether someone or something is best often work.

USING SOURCES

The remix of the impossible argument calls for the integration of sources, and yet I gave no instruction about how this should be done.

If you did it, how did you do it? When the purpose of the writing and the needs of the audience are driving the experience, I find even relatively inexperienced writers have little trouble figuring out how to integrate a source into their argument.

One might argue, for example, that according to a Google Internet dictionary search, a sandwich is defined as "An item of food consisting of two pieces of bread with meat, cheese, or other filling between them, eaten as a light meal." While a hot dog does consist of a bread-like substance surrounding meat, even if a hot dog bun can be defined as bread (which is debatable), it is a single piece of bread, therefore, a hot dog is not a sandwich.

The source is clear in the context of the argument. In order to get a definition of a sandwich, the author has turned to a possible authority on sandwiches.

Citation is a tool to inform the reader where supporting information and sources come from. This helps the audience judge the credibility and appropriateness of the sources and allows others to go back and check our work.

Different occasions, different audiences, require different approaches to sourcing. These approaches evolve all the time. When I was in college, the Internet as a widely available resource didn't exist. Now millions of people carry a connection to the Internet on their bodies all day long.

In English classes, Modern Language Association (MLA) style is the dominant citation scheme. American Psychological Association (APA) style is used in education, psychology, and other sciences.

Chicago style is used in business and fine arts.

In academic writing, citations are more formal because the places where academic writing is published require a uniform system so people who are going to make use of those publications don't have to worry about making those choices.

When writing for print media, you're expected to give as much information as the audience needs to evaluate the credibility of the information at the time of reading, as they're very unlikely to go looking for themselves. Journalists must keep their sources organized in case someone does question an aspect of the story, and are often asked to demonstrate the accuracy to their editors prior to publication.

If you're publishing on the Internet, the expectation is that you will link your sources directly to what you're citing, while including any relevant information in the text itself.

Look at how what you're reading handles sources, and emulate those practices. When you cite sources, keep your audience and purpose in mind. What information do they need in order to be persuaded? What is the authority that makes the source trustworthy? Put that in the text.

If you think about sources from your audience's point of view, you can't go wrong in giving them the information about your sources they need.

This includes teachers who want you to use MLA or APA or Chicago style. Yes, the specifics can seem tricky or arcane, but once you understand *why* you're citing something, *how* to cite it becomes much easier.

I once knew MLA style backward and forward, but over time, as I've written for publications with different guidelines, the rules of the different citation schemes have become jumbled in my brain. Fortunately, the answers are easily accessible thanks to that miracle machine in my pocket.

Try not to think about citing sources as a minefield of rules you have to tiptoe through in order to keep from running afoul of the authorities, like a teacher, editor, or publisher, who are there to enforce an orderly system. Sources are part of the raw material of your writing. They're something to be used, not just tracked or listed.

Citing the work of others that we reference in our own writing is a matter of ethics: giving credit where it's due is the right thing to do. Intentionally taking credit for the work of others is wrong.

It's also a sign of respect for the audience to leave them as informed as possible and provide them access to additional resources on your subject.

Integrating sources is nothing to fear. The sources are there to work for you, rather than the other way around.

You've Got to Do This!

(Passion Argument)

If we're lucky, at some point we're entirely captured by something new—an idea, an activity, a person, an experience. In fact, we're so excited by it, we can't help but try to spread the word, an evangelist for this new thing we love.

Passion and enthusiasm can be very persuasive. Excitement can be contagious; if you can convey your excitement to your audience, they may give your passion a try. It may not stick, but at least you've got a potential convert.

In the last month, I've had people attempt to convince me to try the following: yoga, cooking with an instant pot, CrossFit, and going vegetarian.

Thus far, none of them have succeeded, because while I believed they believed they benefitted from whatever they were trying to get me to do, their arguments were too vague, like, "It's just awesome" (an instant pot) or "It gives me energy" (both yoga and CrossFit).

No one was able to tell me why *I* should do it, how *I* would benefit from embracing their passion.

Your goal in this experience is to induce your audience to want to try your passion by showing them how they would benefit.

AUDIENCE

Your audience is curious and open to new experiences, but they aren't going to say yes to something new just because you mentioned its existence. They need convincing.

Facts and figures may be useful, but ultimately this audience is going to respond to how well you target their needs with a strong and persuasive emotional appeal built on your passion.

PROCESS

1. Identify your passion.
What's the thing you keep saying people need to do? Like, I've got these running shoes called Newtons that changed my life because a woman at the shoe store who specializes in matching people to the right running shoe watched me run and said I should try them. I was instantly faster (not fast, but faster), and what had been occasional knee tendinitis disappeared completely.

For a while, I evangelized for Newtons, but then I realized I'd made a mistake, because Newtons are not meant for everyone's feet and running stride, and started evangelizing for people to go to shoe stores that have experts who can match you with the right shoe.

What are you convinced everyone else must at least try?

2. Consider your passion.
Why are you passionate about your passion? How do you benefit? How is your life enhanced? One way of assessing this is to consider your life before and after your passion. In the early days of digital video recorders, I was a hard-core TiVo evangelist, explaining to people that my existence could be measured in terms of BTiVo

versus ATiVo (before and after TiVo). Being able to call up whatever show I wanted *and* skip through commercials? Old hat now,
but incredible in the early 2000s.

Be as concrete and specific about how your passion enhances
your life as possible. Don't even think about your audience yet;
concentrate on your own experience.

3. Write your down draft.

This is one of those pieces where there's no definite model or template you can find and copy. You'll have to build your own structure as you go. This means first getting as much material as you
can down on the page.

You know it's an argument, and you're trying to be persuasive, so
you want to muster as many possible bits of persuasion as possible.
You'll sort through them later, keeping and honing the best ones.

4. Figure out what you've done.

Now that you've unleashed your passion on the page, it's time to
think about how to translate it for your audience. You've captured
how your passion feels to you. How do you now translate this to
your audience? What are their needs? What will they know about
your passion? What attitudes do they have regarding your passion?

Who is a good target audience for your passion? Identify them
and any relevant traits or attitudes they hold, and write to them
directly.

5. Write a complete draft.

Considering what you've written and what you've discovered
about your audience, shape the down draft into a more focused
and structured argument that communicates your passion in a
way that induces your audience to give it a try.

6. *Test your draft.*

Find someone who is either in your target audience or willing to temporarily adopt the attitudes and viewpoints of your target audience to read your draft and give it a rating on a ten-point scale where one means they'd rather listen to ABBA's greatest hits as sung by a murder of shrieking crows than give your passion a try, and ten means they're starting a new religion in order to worship your passion.

Ask them what they find most and least persuasive about your argument.

7. *Revise, edit, polish.*

Based on your audience's feedback, improve your argument. Edit and polish the manuscript because of what you'll be doing in step 9.

8. *Title.*

Finding a title that illuminates your subject and conveys the depths of your passion (without overselling by too much) should cap off the effort.

9. *Share your passion with the world.*

Find an outlet where you can share your passion. If it's a product, this might be a review where the product is sold. Or you could do it via social media. I've heard tales of people actually making money peddling stuff on this thing called Instagram, whatever that is.

REFLECT

How does the fact of your passion affect your argument? On the one hand, our passions can drive us to become more knowledge-able about what we're advocating. On the other hand, our passions can also blind us to information that challenges our passions. In this case, passion isn't a big problem because the point of the argument is to be passionate, but there may be other occasions where it proves more persuasive to appear dispassionate.

Can you think of writing you've done where dispassion was the right choice?

REMIX

Find or take a single picture that you feel captures your passion in all its intensity. Add some kind of slogan, and you've got yourself a print advertisement. Try it.

Why Am I So Angry and What Can I Do about It?

(Problem/Solution Argument)

It's possible that I'm a malcontent, but I seem to move through life finding lots of things I wish were different. This very book is a result of that. I wasn't entirely happy with the ways other books discussed writing and writing assignments, so I decided to write one of my own that better reflects what I believe in.

Rather than simply being a malcontent, writing an analytical argument about the thing you hate may be a way of better understanding this thing that bothers you while also possibly helping you find a solution to this problem.

There are two versions of this experience: one for those who find themselves currently actively engaged in schooling, and one for those who do not.

VERSION 1: SCHOOL EDITION

Because I've spent many years teaching college, I'm familiar with the kinds of things students are discontented with, like 8:00 a.m. classes. Personally, I like 8:00 a.m. classes, but students look on them as a form of cruel and unusual punishment. They figure they can't do anything about the existence of 8:00 a.m. classes except hope to schedule their own classes during other times.

But what if you could persuade those who do have power to change the thing you hate? What if those who hate 8:00 a.m. classes could convince the people who schedule things like 8:00 a.m. classes that 8:00 a.m. classes shouldn't exist, not because students hate them, but because they do not help fulfill the mission of the institution that schedules 8:00 a.m. classes?

Tackling a problem that shows itself in your own day-to-day life is your next writing-related problem.

Something is not as it should be, and you wish it were different.

AUDIENCE

You are writing for the someone (or someones) who has the power to make the change you seek.

PURPOSE

You want to persuade. But remember, this is not the persuasion of a small child throwing a tantrum until the authority figure gives in. You need to convince your audience that this change is in *everyone's* best interest, not just your own.

PROCESS

1. Feel the hate.
Let loose all the dislike you feel about anything school related. Visualize your day. What are the problems?* What could be better?

---

* For me? Parking. Always parking. Why is there never anywhere for me to park?

Write down everything you can think of, no matter how trivial it might seem, but try to focus on policies and procedures rather than individuals. You're supposed to be in school to learn things and prepare for the future you desire. What stands in the way between you and learning?

2. Find your focus.
From your list, pick an item that seems important to you that also might impact others. It should be something that, if you can solve it, will have a positive impact on the school (or beyond).

3. Consider your audience choices.
What are all the different groups that are affected by this problem? List them. There will be many. We call these people "stakeholders." Which one seems both persuadable and able to make change? This is your audience.

4. Analyze your audience.
Which decision maker(s) are you going to write to? Why have you chosen them? Consider your audience's needs, attitudes, and knowledge regarding your subject.

5. Make your case that a problem exists.
Write an argument that describes and illustrates the problem to the best of your ability without relying on any additional sources. This is only based on your experience, but remember what you know about your audience. What can you say that will persuade them to agree with you that this is a problem worthy of their attention?

You are not complaining. While you are working, feel free to feel your feelings and vent to anyone who will listen, but remember that, in the end, that venting is a pressure release, not an effective method of persuading an audience to take action to help solve the problem.

6. *Improve your case.*

What additional information and research will help improve your argument that this is a problem? What do you need to prove to your audience to be convincing, and what kind of proof do you need to find? Are your sources convincing and authoritative? Maybe you've got a good case, but for a different audience than you first settled on. Should you switch audiences? Maybe you should seek out some test audiences to see how you're doing.

7. *Create a solution.*

As you research your problem, you will likely also find information on possible solutions. You probably have a few ideas of your own as well. What would be a good solution to this issue? How will you convince your audience that it's a good solution?

8. *Draft, revise, edit.*

Now that you've done all this thinking, planning, and research, write a solution to this problem targeted toward your specific audience.

Revision will likely happen even as you draft and your thinking clarifies, but of course if an idea arrives that requires you to rethink something earlier, such as your choice of audience, you'll need to revise accordingly. If you are connected to your material and considering your audience, your instincts will tell you if something seems off target. Listen to those instincts, and don't shy away from digging in and fixing something you think needs it.

9. *Title.*

A title will be especially important here. One technique to consider may be the use of a title and subtitle where the title introduces the subject but primarily functions to interest the reader, and the subtitle clarifies the specific purpose of the piece.

"It's Too Early to Learn: The Importance of Sleep in Academic Achievement."

VERSION 2: LIFE EDITION

In the town where I live, they spent many months and many dollars remaking one of the main roads that runs north to south, going from two lanes in each direction to three lanes, with a big, raised median in the middle. We were promised it would enhance our lives, and to some degree it worked, allowing cars to move more freely, except at a couple of intersections, where they made the left turn lanes branching off the main three lanes too short.

Because of this, traffic often backs up as people are waiting in a lane that should be moving because they don't have enough room to get into the turn lane.

I don't know what it says about me that this makes me irrationally upset every time it causes me a delay, but it does. I want my town to remedy this situation.

This will be your task in this assignment: something is not as it should be and you wish it were different.

AUDIENCE

You are writing for the someone (or someones) who has the power to make the change you seek.

PURPOSE

You want to persuade. But remember, this is not the persuasion of a small child throwing a tantrum until the authority figure gives in. You need to convince your audience that this change is in *everyone's* best interest, not just your own.

PROCESS

1. Feel the hate.

Let loose all the dislikes you have about the way the world operates around you. Visualize your day. What are the problems? What could be better? Maybe it's something at work or even in your own household. Write down everything you can think of, no matter how trivial it might seem, but try to focus on policies and procedures rather than individuals. You're moving through your day-to-day life, trying to achieve certain goals. What prevents you from achieving those goals?

2. Find your focus.

From your list, pick an item that seems important to you and also might impact others. It should be something that, if you can solve it, will have a positive impact on the world beyond yourself.

3. Consider your audience choices.

What are all the different groups affected by this problem? List them. There will be many. We call these people "stakeholders." Which one seems both persuadable and able to make change? This is your audience. In my case, maybe I want to rally the public to the cause. Or would it be better to petition the town council directly, since they're the ones who have to ultimately make the change happen?

4. Analyze your audience.
Which decision maker(s) are you going to write to? Why have you chosen them? Consider your audience's needs, attitudes, and knowledge regarding your subject.

5. Make your case that a problem exists.
Write an argument that describes and illustrates the problem to the best of your ability without relying on any additional sources. This is only based on your experience, but remember what you know about your audience. What can you say that will persuade them to agree with you that this is a problem worthy of their attention?

You are not complaining. While you are working, feel free to feel your feelings and vent to anyone who will listen, but remember that in the end that venting is a pressure release, not an effective method of persuading an audience to take action to help solve the problem

6. Improve your case.
What additional information and research will help improve your argument that this is a problem? What do you need to prove to your audience to be convincing, and what kind of proof do you need to find? Are your sources convincing and authoritative? Maybe you've got a good case, but for a different audience than you first settled on. Should you switch audiences? Maybe you should seek out some test audiences to see how you're doing.

7. Create a solution.
As you do research into your problem, you will likely also find information on possible solutions. You probably have a few ideas of your own as well. What would be a good solution to this issue? How will you convince your audience that it's a good solution?

8. Draft, revise, edit.

Now that you've done all this thinking, planning, and research, write a solution to this problem targeted toward your specific audience.

Revision will likely happen even as you draft and your thinking clarifies, but of course if an idea arrives that requires you to rethink something earlier, such as your choice of audience, you'll need to revise accordingly. If you are connected to your material and considering your audience, your instincts will tell you if something seems off target. Listen to those instincts, and don't shy away from digging in and fixing something you think needs it.

9. Title.

A title will be especially important here. One technique to consider may be the use of a title and subtitle where the title introduces the subject but primarily functions to interest the reader, and the subtitle clarifies the specific purpose of the piece.

"I Can't Drive 45 (Mph): The Dangers of Restricted Traffic Flow Caused by Inadequate Turn Lanes."

REFLECT

How'd that feel? One of the things you should experience in doing this kind of writing is the sense of your growing expertise. You will know much more about your issue at the end than at the beginning of the process.

In the larger world, this is how knowledge is built. You aren't hitting the reset button after every bit of work you produce. The process never ends. Each act builds on the last until, without notic-ing, you seem to possess some real expertise on a subject.

Take a minute to list the things you know now, having written your argument, that you didn't know before.

Do you see any of this knowledge applying to other aspects of your life? Why? How?

REMIX

Same problem, different stakeholders. Pick another audience you might need to persuade. You don't need to rewrite the entire argu-ment, but in a short piece of writing describe any changes you might have to make to be persuasive to this different audience.

Do you need new or different evidence? Should the structure change? What about tone?

FAILURE

Failure is often treated like a dirty word, but it's one writers should embrace.

I often tell students that writing is an extended exercise in fail-ure. After they are done with their looks of horror, I explain what I mean.

In my head, I have the world's greatest novel that would emo-tionally devastate readers to the point where all other writers would simply give up writing novels.

This very book, once again in my head, could transform the way we think about learning how to write, just as long as I approach the page in a way that communicates the vision I hold in my head.

Inevitably, something happens between my head and the page, and the power of my vision is diminished, and yet one hopes there's enough of the remaining energy to make the final result worthwhile.

Failure is inevitable in writing, because regardless of what we've done, we're always capable of achieving more. Even if we maxed out our abilities on a particular project, having done so means we have the potential to do even better next time.

When it comes to learning to write, the best thing we can do is embrace the idea that no matter how much experience we have, we are all novices. Writing will always be hard, and there's no magical cutoff when we can no longer learn from our experiences.

Ernest Hemingway once said, "We're all apprentices in a craft where no one ever becomes a master."

William Zinsser, author of one of the best-selling writing books of all time, on what it was like for him to write: "It was hard and lonely, and the words seldom just flowed."

I've got a million of these. Annie Dillard, Pulitzer Prize winner: "I do not so much write a book as sit up with it, as with a dying friend."

Embracing failure requires two things: (1) believing that we are our own best judges of what is or is not successful, even if someone else disagrees, and (2) being honest with ourselves about not only the quality and effectiveness of our writing, but the effort we're putting into the work itself.

Our results will inevitably lag behind our intentions, but if we're putting in the work, we will improve.

Failure is a great teacher. It's no reason to feel defeated, particularly when measured against our own standards.

It's encouragement to try again.

What Do You Want to Say?

(Finding Your Own Argument)

When I teach my classes, during the semester I ask students to keep track of possible topics for a researched argument essay. If our best writing comes when we're writing about subjects we're passionate and knowledgeable about, I figure it makes sense to give my students as much leeway as possible to find a topic for themselves.

I've taught thousands of students, and they tend to come up with subjects I could never imagine myself.

Because the arguments are personal and unique, I can recall many of them even years later.

I remember one essay on how the use of profanity in hip-hop music is *integral* to the art form itself. Another essay argued for a law requiring veterinary hospitals to report instances of all suspected animal abuse to child and family services agencies because of a high correlation between animal abuse and domestic violence.

A student once argued for the benefits of having a midlife crisis. Another was so convincing about the negative psychological effects of Instagram that I've avoided ever signing up for the service. In that same vein, a student argued that magazines should publish uncorrected versions of every picture they digitally alter so people can see how bodies and faces really look. I don't think it would be legal to compel such a thing, but it was a fascinating argument about the impact of seeing so many unrealistic portrayals of the human form in our media.

Not to get all sentimental, but because of the nature of my work teaching writing, it's possible I've learned more from my students than they've learned from me.

For this experience, find your own argument. Write it for an audience.

AUDIENCE

Your audience can be whomever you want it to be, but it must be a specific audience. Your argument may appeal to people beyond your audience (many of my students' efforts weren't targeted at me), but it will be written with a particular group—with a particular set of needs, attitudes, and knowledge—in mind.

PROCESS

1. Brainstorm possible topics.
One way to do this is to consider the things you're interested in, list them, and see what comes to mind as you think of them. An argument isn't going to pop into your head. The student who wrote about the psychological dangers of Instagram listed all the things they did on a particular day and noticed the significant amount of time spent on the platform. This led to doing some initial research, which triggered a problem and argument.

Your reflections on some of the experiences in this book may be useful here. For example, the reflection on the ethical dilemma considers how difficult it may be to stand up to a boss or supervisor who is telling someone to do something ethically troubling. There could be a topic exploring whether or not employees need more rights and protections when it comes to blowing the whistle on their superiors.

The "Why Should I Trust This?" experience on understanding and evaluating sources raises a question as to whether social media platforms like Facebook and Twitter should seek to police content that is purposefully created to sow false information. If you completed the rhetorical analysis of a commercial, how do you feel about the culture that is being reinforced by the ad?

Personally, it bothers me that so many people expect their jobs to be generally miserable, and I suspect that's at least in part because that's the message promoted by ads for beer. There's probably something in that feeling.

If nothing excites you on that front, go looking. Read other people's arguments. Watch one of those television shows where people argue with each other. Figure out something you want to express to the world in a way that will get them to agree with you.

2. Develop your topic.

Once you have an area or topic of interest, do some research. Dig around and see what other people might be saying, in an effort to help you spur your own thinking.

I wanted to understand if people really hated their jobs or, even better, to understand the difference between people who like their work and those who don't. This directed me to research by the Gallup polling organization about happiness among college graduates. The study showed that people who were "engaged" in their work were 4.6 times more likely to be defined as "thriving" in terms of their personal well-being.

In other words, if you like your job, you're much more likely to be happy in life.

"Hmm . . . ," I thought.

Dig around until you get to your own "hmm" moment.

3. Develop an organizing question.

One thing you may have noticed is that just about every writing experience in this book is organized around a question. If you can find an interesting question, you have an organizing idea around which to write.

My question regarding school and work became: What happens in college that leads to a future life of happiness at work and happiness with life in general?

The Gallup research provided an answer. The most important single experience associated with "engagement" in one's job, according to their survey, is having "had a mentor who encouraged me to pursue my goals and dreams."

Double "hmm."

Questions that drove some of my students' topics were:

How do we reduce incidents of domestic violence?
Why does Instagram make me sad?
What is art?

Any question that keeps the thinking momentum going is a good one.

4. Do additional, more systematic research.

You've been researching this whole time, but once you have a good question, your focus will be improved as you go looking for specific sources to answer specific questions.

Your main question will spawn additional questions. For example, as part of my thinking about work and happiness, I wanted to find out what kind of impact money has on happiness. I discovered many studies saying that once income reaches a certain threshold, making more money does not increase happiness.

The student working on the domestic-violence topic found a

study that connected domestic violence to violence against companion animals. Often animal abuse was a precursor to harming others in the home.

This stage is for gathering as much valid, reliable information that pertains to your question as possible. Resist judging whether it will be useful. You never know until you put the final polish on the final draft.

5. Refine your question into something answerable with an argument.

A question like "How do we reduce incidents of domestic violence?" points us more toward an informative piece of writing rather than an argument. The student altered the question to, "What should we be doing to prevent domestic violence that we're not doing now?"

My question about college and happiness at work took a similar turn: "What should colleges do to increase the likelihood that students will one day be engaged in their jobs?"

6. Draft.

If you've gone through many of this book's experiences so far, you're probably expecting something about audience analysis in this spot, but I find this type of argument frequently first requires some drafting to help figure out who the audience *should* or *could* be.

You can choose your audience and try to write for them, but often too much thinking still needs to happen to have a firm idea of who you want to write for. Much of it depends on what you want your audience to do with your argument, which means figuring out what you can argue effectively.

In writing about what happens in college to affect future job engagement and overall well-being, I wasn't sure if I wanted to write for students, schools, parents, or even give my question a twist and write for employers, under the theory that they want to be on the lookout for students who have had particular experiences because they'll be happier and therefore better employees.

7. Assess your draft and consider the audience.
Here's where you can think about the intersection between your most convincing argument and the audience that can effect the kind of change you think will help improve the status quo.

The student working on domestic violence and animal abuse decided to write for police departments, to encourage better information sharing between animal control and the regular officers when animal abuse is suspected.

In my case, I had a key bit of research from that Gallup poll: according to the survey data, people are 4.6 times more likely to be "thriving" in terms of their overall well-being if they are "engaged" at work. Being fulfilled in one's job apparently plays a huge role in being happy. The poll suggested that the single greatest individual factor for being engaged in future work is if a college graduate had a mentor in college who encouraged them to pursue their hopes and dreams while there.

Even after a draft, I was torn about whether I should write for students, encouraging them to seek out those experiences, or faculty, encouraging them to create more opportunities that correlate to future well-being for students.

Ultimately, I chose to write for faculty, both because I belong to that group and because I felt the bigger problem wasn't student desire for these experiences but aspects of school structures that make it difficult to give students the kind of mentoring they benefit from and that faculty enjoy.

8. Revise.

Now that you have an answer to the question and an audience in mind, revise the argument. In some cases, this will mean starting over with a fresh document.

Regardless, now that you've done all this thinking and have the audience and argument in mind, this revision should be much more targeted.

9. Assess the new draft.

If you think outside readers will be helpful—they usually are—find some. Craft some questions you'd like them to answer about the draft. What are you still debating in terms of your own approach? What sorts of things do you want them to weigh in on? After they've had a chance to react to the piece, use your readers to help give you additional insight into what you're trying to accomplish.

10. Edit and polish.

You know the drill by now.

11. Title.

Always important, but especially vital this time.

REFLECT

Take a minute to appreciate that you made something that didn't exist before. This isn't a research paper that repeats a bunch of stuff others have said previously. It's a work by a unique intelligence that would not exist if *you* had not created it.

It's kind of fun to think about.

OTHER WRITING EXPERIENCES

Just because these experiences are filed under "other," don't think of them as insignificant. In fact, a couple of these are the most difficult experiences in the entire book.

Knowing how to write a proposal ("May I?") is a particular type of argument that is highly adaptable to any occasion, be it asking for money or even applying for a job. Being able to anticipate the needs of your audience is a vital skill for success here.

Writing a well-turned joke requires both creativity and a ruthless attention to precision in using language.

The conflict and solution letters not only have a practical purpose in helping assess and remedy a personal issue; they also allow for the practice of a key writing skill, rhetorical sensitivity, which is particularly relevant when making arguments with an eye toward convincing audiences to act.

Two experiences require the crafting of advice, something many of us are inclined to do but without as much thought as is required here.

The profile and the tribute are similar, except one is about a stranger, and the other is about someone you already know well. The short imagined monologue is proof that anyone can write something funny.

"The Right Word vs. the Almost Right Word" is an exercise in thinking about sentences and can be repeated over and over again.

These are experiences that allow you to see how well you can transfer what you learn from one experience to another.

May I...?

(Proposal)

A proposal is a document that seeks permission.

Prior to writing this book, I submitted a proposal to the publisher, trying to convince it to publish this book in exchange for money.

It worked! In order to convince Penguin to part with its money and put the necessary time and resources into producing and distributing this book, I had to answer several questions (and subquestions) to its satisfaction.

1. Is this a book worthy of publication?

   A. Does it look like it will be a good book?

   B. Is it sufficiently different from other books targeting similar audiences?

2. Is this a book *we* specifically should publish?

   A. Is it the kind of book we can successfully market and distribute?

   B. Is it a book on which we can reasonably expect to turn a profit?

3. Is the person who is proposing to write this book capable of writing this book and engaging in other activities necessary to ensure a reasonable chance of success?

A. What is the background the author brings to the task?

B. What sort of author "platform" does the author possess that may help promote the book?

To answer these questions, I had to present an argument as to the necessity and relevancy of a book like this as well as my background and qualifications. I submitted a sample of the book I intended to write. When submitting a proposal, all the power rests with the audience, as it has the authority to say yes or no to what the author is proposing.

It's nerve-racking, to be honest, but highly gratifying when someone says yes to a proposal.

Being able to convince someone to say yes to something you want to do is a highly valuable and adaptable skill you are going to practice with this experience.

I often ask for proposals from students who are working on researched writing. They write to me to tell me what they're planning and how they're going about their work. This also gives me an opportunity to offer some advice as we're on the journey of the assignment.

And even more important, it gives the students a chance to prove to themselves that they're ready to take the next step. Finishing the proposal was the only way I knew I could start to write this book.

AUDIENCE

A proposal is generally written for a person with the power to make a decision. A grant proposal is written for someone who gets to decide whether to fund a project or person. A pitch to a publication is looking for a go-ahead to write a piece in exchange for compensation. Maybe you want to convince your significant other to take a vacation in a specific locale. Maybe you want to convince an employer to change a policy at work.

A successful proposal is a prerequisite for moving forward. In some cases, a proposal may undergo several rounds of revision prior to approval, as the person with the decision-making power requests additional information in order to be reassured that yes is the correct answer.

Whoever your audience is, you'll want to be sensitive to what it's going to take to convince them to say yes to what you're proposing.

PROCESS

1. Determine goal and audience.

What do you want to propose and who do you want to propose it to? Make sure what you want and your audience are appropriately matched. You should only propose something to an audience that has the power to make it happen. I can show my book proposals to my mother and get a yes any time I want, but she doesn't own or run a publishing company.

2. Analyze audience and occasion.

To be persuasive you will not need to convince your audience that saying yes will be good for you; you have to convince them that saying yes is good for *them*. Why is it in *their* interest to say yes?

Understanding this requires in-depth analysis of their needs, attitudes, and knowledge. Think of the questions they have about what you're proposing and how you can answer those questions to their satisfaction. A proposal is an argument with claims and evidence.

3. Create an outline.

If you are writing a specific proposal for a specific audience, you may be able to find a template online. Grant proposals, in which you ask for money, often require you to follow very specific guidelines, and any deviation can result in being disqualified.

If there isn't a specific template, go back your audience and their questions. The outline for my book proposal followed a series of questions.

1. What is the book being proposed?

2. Why does the book meet the needs of the marketplace?

3. Who is the audience for the book?

4. Who is the author of the book? (And why should we trust him?)

5. How will the book be structured and what will it contain?

6. What is an example of the content?

To draft the proposal, list the questions you need to answer for your audience.

4. Draft the proposal.

Once you have a good outline of questions to answer, write the draft, answering the questions. Simple in concept, difficult in execution. This really requires you to put yourself in your audience's shoes every step of the way. Any objection they might have to saying yes you have to identify and knock down, hopefully before they even think of it.

5. Test, revise, edit, polish, title.

Depending on what you're proposing, you'll want to find someone who can help give additional perspective on how you're doing in answering the questions your audience will have.

In my case, I have the benefit of a literary agent who handles dozens and dozens of proposals per year. If you're proposing something for your workplace, find someone who has had supervisory responsibilities. If it's a grant proposal, try to find someone who has successfully secured a grant.

Their experience and perspective will help. If you can't find a person with exactly relevant experience, find someone who you think is capable of assuming the mind-set of the person to whom you're making your proposal.

As you likely suspect, a high degree of polish is extremely important in this type of writing. You don't want someone who is inclined to say yes to tip at the last second toward no because of some typo or other easily fixable mistake.

The title should be straightforward and informative, fitting for a utilitarian document such as a proposal.

REFLECT

The question-based outline is a handy technique to use in a lot of different writing contexts, particularly when you have a highly defined objective and very specific audience.

It can be harder to see how one would work for other, less clearly defined genres, but the questions being answered for the audience can be reverse engineered out of just about anything you write.

Take one of your pieces from another experience and see if you can identify the questions you're answering with each paragraph or section. Looking at the question outline can be a good tool for thinking about structure as you revise. If the sequencing of the questions seems off, switch them around until the flow works to meet audience needs.

Make Me Laugh

(Jokes)

In the late 1970s there was a very simple, very straightforward game show called *Make Me Laugh*.

The premise was that one at a time, for sixty seconds each, three comics would get a shot at making the contestant laugh. For every second the contestant didn't laugh, he or she would receive one dollar.

Yes, the maximum prize was $180. This was the 1970s. A McDonald's hamburger was a dime, and students still wrote their assignments with quill and parchment.

Perhaps the most successful comedian on *Make Me Laugh* was a guy known as the Unknown Comic, who performed with a paper grocery sack over his head with holes for his eyes and mouth. He told terrible jokes that dated back decades, but he could sometimes get a laugh by twirling the bag on top of his head to reveal a funny face drawing on the back, the surprise of which would instantly crack up the contestant.

(It's funnier to watch than to hear it described. Check it out online.)

It is very hard not to laugh—in shock, in embarrassment, or genuine humor—when someone in front of your face is trying to make you laugh.

It is much harder to make someone laugh when they are merely reading your joke, rather than having it be performed.

The latter is your task. This may be the hardest thing I've ever asked students to do. It's also the most fun.

EXPERIENCE

Write five jokes that would be appropriate for a host to deliver on a topical late-night show (*The Daily Show, Full Frontal with Samantha Bee, Saturday Night Live Weekend Update, Last Week Tonight with John Oliver,* etc.)

Note that this work is often best done collaboratively. All of these shows rely on what are called "writers' rooms," which are collaborative spaces where individually talented people are made better by the chance to work with other talented people toward a common goal. Gather a group together to practice this one.

AUDIENCE

Your first audience is the host of the show. You are a member of the writing team and you are going to pitch your jokes for inclusion in the show's monologue. Ultimately, though, the audience is the viewers who tune in.

PROCESS

1. Figure out how jokes work (structure).
How are they structured? Do you see patterns? What makes the jokes that are funny, funny? What is the subject material of their jokes?

2. *Analyze the audience.*

Based on your study of the jokes themselves, how would you describe the audience? What do they like? What do they believe? What are their interests? How old are they? Remember to link your conclusion to your observations from the jokes you've been studying.

3. *Brainstorm.*

Throw out ideas for your team of joke writers to bat around. Get access to a dry-erase board or a way to project a computer screen onto a wall for all to see. What are some funny ideas for jokes? (Not the jokes themselves.) Build on each other's ideas and don't hold back. No judgment, just ideas.

4. *Write rough jokes.*

Try converting your funny ideas into the joke structures you identified earlier.

5. *Try out your jokes.*

Seek out an audience who hasn't been privy to the creation of your jokes. Try them out. Ask some of your test audience just to read the jokes. For others, you can try to deliver the jokes as a host would. Does your audience laugh? If yes, the jokes are funny. If not, they are not funny.

6. *Revise the jokes.*

The most effective jokes—as you noticed in your study of the form—use exactly the right word for the moment and often are as concise and tight as possible. They also rely on rhythms, almost like poetry. Go back to the example jokes you thought were best and see if you can polish your jokes so they work in similar ways.

REFLECT

That was really difficult, wasn't it? If you got anything other than blank stares from your audience, you've done tremendously well. If you got blank stares, you've experienced what every comedian in the world has been through the first time they tried writing and telling jokes.

Why, do you think, is joke writing so hard? What are the skills that go into writing jokes? If this was the kind of career you wanted to pursue, what sorts of things should you be doing to train for that eventuality?

Think of it this way: If your goal is to become a concert violinist, there are things you're going to do to achieve that goal. What if your goal is to write jokes? What should you be doing?

Do you have something in mind for your own future? What are the experiences, what is the knowledge, that stand between you and what you might like to do?

COLLABORATION

There is a paradox at the heart of writing, in that as we're doing it, it is largely a solo pursuit, and yet, at the same time, we can see all writing as essentially collaborative.

Writing without an audience to respond to you is like the old parable about a tree falling in the forest: if no one is around, does it make a sound? Only when writing intersects with an audience do we create meaning. That is a collaborative act. The meaning would not exist without the work of both the writer and the audience. Sometimes those meanings are different from what the original author intended, which highlights how difficult collaboration can be.

Sometimes that disconnect is the fault of the writer failing to carefully craft their message. Other times, though, it is the reader who is not holding up their end of the bargain and is misinterpreting a message by not reading closely enough or even by being fogged by bias. The collaboration breaks down when either one of the parties doesn't fulfill their responsibilities.

One of the things I like most about trying to write humor (as in the jokes experience) is that the audience feedback is instantaneous and cannot be faked. Either people laugh or they don't. Their laughter is the audience fulfilling its part of the collaboration. Occasionally, a silent audience can be blamed on the audience itself, but almost always the fault is found in the writer. There's something very pure about this, knowing when you've succeeded and when you haven't.

Writers and their editors have an inherently collaborative relationship. Ideally, the editor is focused on helping the writer best express their message, which requires the editor to understand the writer's intent, and the writer to be open to accepting the editor's feedback.

And there are types of writing where even the writing itself is collaborative. Technical writing often involves collaboration in putting together long and complex documents where different parts are farmed out to different people. In this kind of work, the collaboration tends to require a lot of upfront planning, after which individuals go off to fulfill their part of the project.

Writing for television often requires a blend of collaborative styles. There is always someone in charge, a host (as in a late-night show) or a "showrunner," who must manage a team of writers. In some cases, like in a TV drama, a season-long arc will be established, and then the writers go off to craft individual episodes, which are brought back to the group for feedback, which leads to revision. Ultimately, the person in charge makes the final decision.

Other times, writers will literally be in a writers' room collaborating in real time to generate ideas or propose particular jokes. Participating effectively in this kind of atmosphere requires a healthy mix of ego and humility. One must be confident enough to throw ideas into the mix, and humble enough to accept when someone else's idea is better. Not easy to do.

I find thinking of writing as collaborative makes the act of writing considerably less lonely. It can be highly motivating to know that our work is going into the world and other people will get to make something of it for themselves.

Are You Trying to
Make Me Angry?

(Conflict Letter)

Interpersonal conflict is inevitable. Even if you are the nicest person in the world, surrounded by other incredibly nice and courteous people, conflict will arise, perhaps taking the form of a certain amount of annoyance about how nice everyone is.

For this experience, you're going to really let loose on someone with whom you're having a conflict. It may be constant or periodic, large or small.

It may be that your spouse, the love of your life, whom you will be spending the rest of your days with, to the point where you hope one day to pass away side by side in your shared nursing-home bed has a habit of using half of a Splenda packet and then trying to save the second half of the packet by twisting the top closed, but because the packets are so small, they inevitably reopen, spilling the tiny Splenda crystals onto the counter, thus rendering the saving of the packet moot and irritating you, because now there's also a mess.

Phew. Got a little heated up just thinking about it.

You may have a bigger conflict, which is also fine. The goal here is to really give a piece of your mind to the person you're having the conflict with. It could be a friend, a roommate, a parent, a boss, a coworker—anyone. It could even be a situation where the person with whom you're in conflict is unaware of the problem.

AUDIENCE

You're writing directly to the person with whom you're in conflict. It's a letter.

PROCESS

1. Identify the person with whom you are in conflict and the evidence of that conflict.
What are you mad about? Why does this make you mad? Gather the information and evidence surrounding your conflict.

2. Let 'em have it.
Write the letter telling the person with whom you're in conflict about the conflict, how you're being harmed, and what you want them to do about it. Make sure it's sufficiently clear and detailed so the other person knows what you're talking about.

3. Sigh with satisfaction.
How did that feel? Was it good to get it off your chest? Even though the situation is entirely unchanged, it can still feel good just to unburden yourself on the page.

4. Show your letter to someone else with no relationship to, or stake in, the conflict.
This is very, very important. Under no circumstances should you show your letter to the person with whom you're in conflict or even anyone who may be related to the conflict. Find an impartial,

neutral observer. If there's anything in the letter you'd rather not disclose to this person, feel free to edit it out for these purposes.

Ask this person to try to read it from the perspective of the recipient. If they were the recipient, how would they react to receiving it?

REFLECT

A guess based on my experience: your disinterested reader believes if you sent this letter to the person with whom you're in conflict, the conflict would not only *not* be solved but would intensify, much the same way me exclaiming to my beloved spouse, "For the love all that's holy, either use the whole Splenda packet or throw out the rest!" didn't go over so well.

It is rare to impossible for these sorts of conflicts to be solved by one person using a barrage of accusations to force the other to back down. Even if you have the power or influence to force them to comply with your wishes, you've merely transferred the conflict to the other person, and some kind of larger reckoning or blowup seems inevitable.

Now that you've had a chance to vent a little, it's time to try a different approach, the solution letter.

How Can I Help You Help Me?

(Solution Letter)

As should be clear at this point, the letter you wrote to the person with whom you're having conflict is unlikely to have a positive effect. It would only make things worse, and yet the conflict remains, so it's important to try to do something to address it.

You're going to write another letter, except this time you're going to try to focus on a solution, rather than the problem.

AUDIENCE

The audience is the same as in the conflict letter, though this time you're going to spend more time thinking about them than thinking about yourself.

PROCESS

1. Considering the same conflict, take a step back and look at it from the point of view of the person with whom you're in conflict.

What are their needs in relation to the situation? Why do you think they've adopted the stance or attitudes they hold? Do your best to give them the benefit of the doubt.

What needs are they fulfilling by engaging in the behavior that seems to be causing a conflict with you?

2. Now spend some time thinking about your needs.
What is it you need in regard to this situation?

Try not to think about it as something as reductive as, "I need my spouse to stop using Splenda packets so I never have to look at another one in my life." There's nothing inherently wrong with using Splenda packets. My need in this conflict is rooted more in feelings that I'm being tasked with cleaning up after someone who is perfectly capable of cleaning up after herself but for some reason doesn't do it.

In other words, it's not about the Splenda. And, by and large, I don't spend a lot of time cleaning up after my spouse, at least not any more than she cleans up after me. It's just that this thing really bugs me.

I often hear from students about roommate problems. For instance, one person is a night owl and the other an early riser. In this case, both parties have a need to use their shared space in ways that meet their rhythms. If the people in conflict focus on their needs, they may be able to find a win-win solution to the problem.

3. Look for a solution.
Rather than thinking about ending the conflict by getting the other person to do exactly what you want them to do, see if you can find a third way that meets both of your needs. This isn't necessarily a compromise, like it'll be okay if Splenda packets are left on the counter every other day. Often those compromises just make both parties feel crummy.

Try to find a solution, or perhaps a first step toward a solution, that you would feel comfortable proposing to the person with whom you're in conflict.

4. Write a new letter.
This time write a letter practicing maximum "rhetorical sensitivity." Think of your goal as not to let them have a piece of your

mind, but instead to demonstrate how much you've been thinking about things from their perspective. Let them see that you've tried to understand their mind-set.

Structurewise, think about how you may want to open the letter in a way that gets them feeling comfortable, rather than defensive. Then transition to your solution and do your best to explain how you think it will benefit everyone involved. Write to them in a tone that you think you'd respond well to if you were on the receiving end.

5. Test the letter.
If possible, show the letter to the same person who read the previous one. Once again, ask them to put themselves in the other person's shoes. Do they think it will work better than the other letter?

Do they have any suggestions for improvement, either in tone or structure or even in the solution itself?

REFLECT

Some people decide to go ahead and show the letter to the person with whom they're having a conflict. Others use the letter as a template for a conversation. Others take no action. All of the above are acceptable. No one choice is superior. You get to act in the interests of your own well-being.

One thing worth doing at this point is to take a moment to consider your emotional state after drafting each letter. Did you feel different after writing the second letter than after the first? How? Which feeling do you prefer?

If I Knew Then
What I Know Now

(Advice to Your Former Self)

Life brings regrets—it's inevitable. Even the most conscientious person can't avoid mistakes or bad outcomes.

And a lot of the time the negative outcome wasn't even foreseeable, because you didn't know enough to realize something bad was lurking around the corner. I find this is especially true of college. It seems like lots of people assume students know how it's all supposed to work, and yet this often isn't the case.

Just as one example, at the start of college I didn't know you could drop a class, so after getting a very poor grade on the first exam in Econ 101, I had to get almost all As to barely scrape by with a B for the semester. Maybe this was a good learning experience, but maybe I also would've been better off knowing there was some room for a do-over in the college experience.

For this experience, you're going to write to your past self and tell that past self something you know now that you wish you knew then.

AUDIENCE

Your audience is literally you in an earlier time and space. But you should also presume that your circumstances are not entirely unique and are likely shared by others.

PROCESS

1. Identify a bad outcome that could have been avoided.
Remember, it's not a matter of making a smarter choice when the not-so-smart choice led to predictably bad results.

That poor grade on the first exam in Econ 101 might've been predicated on saying yes to an invitation to go a Chinese restaurant at 3:30 p.m. on a Wednesday afternoon the day before the 8:00 a.m. exam and then indulging in several "volcanoes," a rum punch served in a giant ceramic vessel shaped like a volcano, with a flaming shot of rum in the middle. I figured I'd have plenty of time to go home and study that night, before the exam.

This was obviously delusional, and I knew it even at the time.

But not knowing about being able to drop a class was a different deal, a lack of information, not of judgment. We're looking for a situation where you lacked information.

2. Draft a letter to your past self.
Be kind to the person you were. Tell them what you know now that you wish you'd known then, while also telling them how to act upon this new information. Emphasize the benefits of taking a different path. Your past self may need some convincing.

3. Revise, edit, and polish.
You'll want your past self to be impressed with the writer you've become.

REFLECT

Are there times when you've escaped a negative outcome in this kind of situation, even though it easily could've turned out differently? What happened?

REMIX

Write a letter to your future self, reminding that future self of something you'd like to remember about how you looked at the world when you were younger. Getting older doesn't necessarily mean we're improving ourselves every step of the way.

What's something you'd like to hold on to twenty or thirty years from now?

FEEDBACK

If we write, we will receive feedback.

One of the great regrets of my life as a writing teacher is how much time I spent giving students feedback about all the things they were doing wrong in their writing. I did this because it was done to me when I was a student, and it took a number of years for me to realize that for the most part those corrections and criticisms weren't particularly helpful when it came to learning how to write.

Broadly speaking, there are two kinds of feedback: summative and formative.

Summative feedback is focused on evaluation, describing how successful or unsuccessful something is relative to a goal.

At halftime in a game, when the team is losing and a coach launches into the players, saying something like "That was garbage out there! I can't believe what I'm seeing! Missed assignments! Lack of hustle! Terrible! I'm disgusted!," that's summative feedback.

Formative feedback is designed to help the person receiving the feedback do better next time.

When the coach breaks out the game film and instructs the players on what to do if certain situations reoccur in the second half, that's formative assessment.

Grades are obviously summative. By themselves, they do little to suggest what should be done next time around. Just about everyone has experienced the sensation of believing they've done a solid job on a piece of writing, then receiving a grade lower than expected. Summative feedback by itself is not helpful in this kind of situation.

When I was spending a lot of time making these corrections on my students' writing, I suppose I thought this would lead them to "learn from their mistakes." I believe this was a mistaken idea for a couple of reasons. First, because I had also put a grade on the assignment, the grade became the piece of feedback to rule them all, the only thing that mattered.

And, second, my corrections weren't truly formative because I hadn't addressed the underlying conditions that caused the shortcomings. I did not address the "why" of the mistakes, and I did not offer any suggestions for future improvement.

Back to my sports analogy. A player could make an error for a number of reasons. It could be a "mental mistake": in the moment, they forgot the right thing to do. It could be a physical shortcoming: lack of speed or strength. It could be that they never knew the right thing to do to begin with. It could be bad technique.

Or it could just be lack of experience. The first time we try something, the odds that we'll do it optimally are vanishingly small.

Writing is very much like this. For feedback to be useful, it has to provide information the writer can act on in the future. Schools often favor systems designed in ways that discourage this kind of feedback. Workplaces with hierarchies may have similar issues. The goal is to get the work done in the moment, which results in a lot of corrections being made mechanically, rather than utilizing a process to help the employee improve in the future.

Ideally, good and useful feedback comes from above, but this may not always be possible.

When it's not possible or forthcoming, there are some things the writer can do to try to get more formative feedback.

One step is to be reflective about your own writing process. If you only receive summative feedback, you can still go back and evaluate how you went about producing your work. It's possible to read between the lines of summative feedback and build your own formative strategies.

Another step is to seek out the formative feedback you feel you're not receiving. The experiences in this book often include steps where you seek formative feedback coupled with summative feedback. Use the same strategies for your work. You can even approach those who are tasked with giving you feedback for more information.

The key is to be as specific as possible. Approaching a teacher and asking, "Why did I get this grade?," will result in a recitation of all the errors that were already identified. On the other hand, if you notice a particular error, you can ask something like, "I see that you marked (X). Is there anything you think I should do to avoid that in the future?"

When it comes to feedback, it's ultimately up to the writer to decide what is useful and to act upon it and discard the rest. The goal is to become largely self-regulating, capable of making use of any feedback, no matter its source or quality.

It's best when we're getting good, formative feedback from an expert, but there are a lot of situations when this just isn't possible. When it isn't coming, you can always rely on your own ability to reflect upon and better understand your writing.

What Should I Do?

(Advice to Someone Else)

At some point in our lives we run up against a dilemma that seems unsolvable.

This experience is not about those dilemmas. This is about when those dilemmas happen to someone else, when life has handed them something so terrible that they take the desperate step of writing to an advice columnist.

I grew up reading "Ask Ann Landers" and "Dear Abby" in the newspaper, but my contemporary favorites are "Ask Polly" (Heather Havrilesky) and "Dear Prudence" (Daniel Mallory Ortberg). There are also the columns "Dear Sugar" (Cheryl Strayed), "Ask Amy" (Amy Dickinson), "Captain Awkward," and, stretching the definition just a bit, the r/relationships forum on Reddit.

Your job in this case is to be the giver of advice.

AUDIENCE

There are two broad category of audiences for this piece of writing:

1. The person asking for advice.

2. Everyone else who is reading the advice.

You should spend some time considering the needs, attitudes, and knowledge of the person soliciting advice. What are they experiencing and feeling? Why are they feeling those feelings? What risks are they confronting depending on different possible paths forward? One of the pleasures for the uninvolved audience is the feeling of relief and superiority that we don't find ourselves in such a desperate situation. There is no shame in feeling this way, but an advice giver has an ethical and moral obligation to the advice receiver that we can think of as akin to the Hippocratic oath taken by physicians, often summarized as: first do no harm.

But advice columns are also meant for the enjoyment and edification of the wider audience. If this audience wasn't part of the calculation, advice columns wouldn't be so popular.

What to do? What to do?

PROCESS

1. Familiarize yourself with the form.
While there is no strict outline to an advice column, you should be able to identify certain commonalities you should either carry over or have a good reason to reject. For example, most advice columns are written to respond directly to the person asking for advice. What other elements can you identify?

2. Find someone with a problem.
The r/relationship sub-Reddit is a great place to go looking for problems. Some of them are so outlandish as to seem fake, which makes them entertaining but may make it tough to write advice for. Pick one for which you think you might have some wisdom to share.

3. Give advice.
What should this person do? Why should they do it? Write your response as you would an advice column.

4. Run your advice by an audience.
This could be a friend, but you could also post it directly to Reddit. See what kind of response you get.

5. Revise your advice.
Based on the feedback you've received, how would you change your advice? In some cases, it may be a radical shift from suggesting one thing to another. In others, it may be a matter of wording or presentation to make sure the advice is well received.

REFLECT

Something you probably noticed as you perused examples of advice columns is that the vast majority are written by women. Why is this? What does this say about the nature of advice, or about our culture, that even today public advice is primarily a job for women?

If you found advice columns written by men, what are they like? Are they different from those written by women? In what ways? Again, why?

REMIX

When I think about the sorts of problems I've had in my life where I've been trapped between two (or more) bad choices, I find that a series of bad choices, bad luck, or some combination of the two, put me in the situation. If someone had given me advice (and I'd listened to it), I might've avoided heading down the bad path in the first place.

Try writing another advice column, only this time write something seeking to head off the trouble *before* it comes to pass. Rather than addressing the specific advice seeker, think of the audience as a category of people who *may be* prone to falling into bad situations. What advice can you give to prevent the worst from happening?

No, Seriously,
Make Me Laugh

(Short Imagined Monologue)

Many people doubt their ability to write something funny, but in my experience a humorous piece of writing lies within the grasp of every sentient being, with the possible exception of a couple people I won't name (but you can probably guess the type).

At its heart, humor relies on incongruity, the juxtaposition of two (or more) things that don't seem to belong together. In combination, these elements create a kind of friction or disturbance or tension, the resolution of which results in laughter. Think of the mean tweets from Jimmy Kimmel's show, where celebrities read the meanest things others have said about them on Twitter, or the silly walk sketch from *Monty Python*, where a British government bureaucrat is the head of the Ministry of Silly Walks, and the performance of these silly walks is done inside a stuffy, government office. (If you don't know these things, take a minute to find and watch them.)

To write something funny, you don't need to *be* funny; you just need to create a humorous juxtaposition and let the scenario dictate the rest. To help you achieve this, you'll work inside a particular form called the "short imagined monologue."

The short imagined monologue is not unique to the *McSweeney's Internet Tendency* website, but it contains an excellent collection of examples of the form. (To see these, search for "McSweeney's short imagined monologue" and you will see them at the top of the results.)

Some example titles include:

"My Life Might Look Great on Instagram, But Deep Down I'm Actually a Ciranolid Isopod"

"You're Damn Right I'm Comfortable Performing These Exit Row Duties"

"A Bear Explains How to Survive a Bear Attack"

"Covering Teen Wolf: One Coach's Guide"

"Morgan Freeman Buys a Pop-A-Shot Machine"

"Cookie Monster Searches Deep Within Himself and Asks: Is Me Really Monster?"

Just from the titles, we can immediately appreciate the juxtapositions. Instagram is well known for people trying to present a glamorous facade to the world while obscuring the deeper underlying reality. In this case, the reality is not only that life is not as glamorous as an Instagram account makes it out to be, but the account holder also happens to be a member of the crustacean family.

Enthusiasm for sitting in the exit row seems odd, and Morgan Freeman is more known for lending his baritone to important and dramatic narration, not something as mundane as buying a game you find in tricked-out basements and sports bars.

Your goal is to find a juxtaposition and execute a monologue that induces a humorous response from your audience.

AUDIENCE

You are writing for people looking for short, diverting entertainment. They are the type of people who are surfing through Facebook or Twitter, have their attention briefly captured by something, click on the link, and then ingest the experience. You want to hook them and keep them hooked for the duration of your monologue.

PROCESS

1. Identify the juxtaposition.

Through brainstorming, simply let your mind free to consider odd and unexpected things. You can start with something mundane (like sitting in an exit row on a plane), and then find an odd juxtaposition (enthusiasm), or do the opposite and think of something or someone interesting (Morgan Freeman) doing something mundane and out of character (buying a Pop-A-Shot machine).

Many good juxtapositions are born from asking, "What if?" What if *Teen Wolf* were real and not a movie in which a boy turns into a wolf and for some reason is allowed to play high school basketball? Let your mind wander and be inspired. For example, just as I was typing this I thought about *Teen Wolf* and basketball and my brain went like this:

Teen Wolf, basketball, animals playing basketball, *Air Bud* (a movie in which a golden retriever plays basketball), do something with *Air Bud*—what if the dog was caught doing performance-enhancing drugs?

Do I know if that will ultimately pan out into something funny? I do not, but it might, and that's the place to start.

2. Develop the juxtaposition.

Once you have what seems to be a promising juxtaposition, spend some time brainstorming like I did above. What can I do with performance-enhancing drugs and a golden retriever?

What performance would be enhanced? What are golden retrievers know for? Cuteness and friendliness? What if the dog's performance-enhancing drugs made him too cute or too friendly? Maybe he was caught because he grew excess hair and had a terrible shedding problem? What would that look like? What would he do? How would other people react to him?

As you develop your juxtaposition, often a little story or narrative will emerge. The juxtaposition puts something in motion that has structure, moving toward some kind of resolution. Maybe the dog is apologizing or announcing his retirement because he's been caught. I don't know—I'm still just thinking here. Keep thinking of these little bits until you feel like you have some moments for the story.

3. Draft your monologue.

Remember that a monologue is a direct address from a specific speaker, so here is where you want to find a voice for your character. What would a drug-abusing, basketball-playing dog sound like? Would it be funnier to have him sound goofy and frantic or better for him to be subdued and serious, like an entitled basketball star, adding an additional potentially humorous juxtaposition? Maybe I should combine a serious tone with barks and growls.

Look at some of the examples and see how the voice is handled. One of the funniest parts of the Cookie Monster monologue is how beautifully the author (Andy Bryan) captures Cookie Monster's voice, even in the title: "Is Me Really Monster?" Most of us have such a strong visual image of Cookie Monster, and because the voice is so good, that image is conjured entirely through words. That's an amazing feat.

4. Refine your monologue.

Here is where precision of language and specific word choice will be key. If you've done the joke-writing experience, you know how much finding just the right word matters. To really polish something like this may take days. Spend just a little time on it each day, honing the piece, then letting it sit before coming back to it later. You don't want to just hammer away at it for hours on end. Let your brain refresh itself so you come at it with fresh eyes.

One tip is to read the monologue out loud to yourself. A monologue is meant to reflect something spoken, so reciting it will help you hear any awkward spots that need fixing.

5. *Title your monologue.*
As you can see from the examples, the title plays a huge part in the success of the monologue. It should both set the premise and intrigue the audience so they want to see what's inside. It doesn't need to be LOL itself, but it should induce an anticipatory feeling that laughs are ahead.

6. *Test your monologue.*
How you test your monologue is up to you. You could try submitting it to *McSweeney's* or the "Shouts & Murmurs" section of the *New Yorker*, or posting it on social media.

The only way to truly test if something is funny is to trot it out for an audience and see if they laugh. This can be emotionally fraught, but if you connect, it is very fun and satisfying.

REFLECT

This sort of writing requires a very intensive process, particularly in revision. Did you notice how helpful it was to read the work out loud? This is a good strategy for just about any piece of writing, as it helps you slow down your reading and really concentrate on the effect you're having on the audience. If nothing else, it will help you correct small errors that our eyes are likely to gloss over when only reading on-screen or on the page.

REMIX

If you're feeling confident and brave, look for a public forum like an open-mic or comedy showcase where you can read or perform your monologue. If you don't want to be quite that public, do it for a group of friends or family. Before delivering the monologue, practice it by reading it out loud and considering where pauses or emphasis might serve your comedic purposes.

Who Is This Stranger?

(Profile)

If you get to know them, most people have something going on that makes them notable.

This experience is centered around helping your audience understand what is notable about someone else. Your job is to "profile" your subject in a way that allows your audience to get to know them.

To do this, you will become a conduit for information. Your audience has no direct experience with the subject of your profile, so they're relying on you to give a thorough and accurate portrayal. This isn't to say you're responsible for writing your subject's life story—a profile is more of an introduction than the entire tale—but you do want your audience to walk away understanding what makes the person you're profiling an interesting individual.

This will also require expert-level reading like a writer in order to familiarize yourself with the ins and outs, whys and wherefores, of writing a profile.

AUDIENCE

Your audience enjoys hearing about the lives of other people, and so is naturally inclined to start reading a piece they can readily identify as a profile, but at the same time they're looking for interesting stories. Not any old profile will do. Think about capturing their interest and sustaining that interest throughout the profile.

PROCESS

1. Identify the subject and secure cooperation.
The first step is to choose someone to profile. The best plan is to choose someone *you* find interesting, since you can use your own interest to drive your investigations. The things you find fascinating may be interesting to your audience as well. This need not be someone famous or prominent. It just needs to be someone whose life or work you're curious to know more about. Profiles tend to be either general, reflecting interest in this person for who they are, or a microcosm, meaning we're interested in this person because of some aspect of their life or achievements.

You'll need to get their permission to profile them, because you will need to be able to observe and interview them. I suppose it's possible to do this without someone knowing you're observing and interviewing them, but it would take the skills of a master spy to pull it off, so it's easier just to ask someone if they're open to having you dip into their lives for a little bit in order to help other people understand what it's like to be them.

Make sure to be clear about how much time and access you'll need. (Read through the entire process before you begin.) You don't want to get partway through the process, then have them get irritated with how long it's taking and rescind your access.

2. Identify and digest model profiles.
Profiles are easy to find. Magazines, newspapers, and websites publish profiles of people all the time. Find half a dozen examples and

read them. Utilize your skills of response, observation, and analysis to uncover the tricks of the trade for how profiles work.

Audiences bring specific expectations to their reading of profiles. You want to understand those expectations so you can fulfill them. There may be some room for variation, but the interesting part of a profile is usually the subject itself, not how far the writer pushes the boundaries of the form. (Though there are, of course, exceptions.)

You should be able to see how profiles are structured, as well as what sort of information is usually included. For example, many profiles will include some history and background of the subject, as well as what's known as "verbal portraiture," a technique that quickly describes the person in a way that puts a mental picture of them in the audience's mind.

Here is an example of the greatest verbal portraiture in the history of the English language, the opening sentence of Susan Orlean's "Orchid Fever," published in the *New Yorker* and later expanded into a book (*The Orchid Thief*) and even adapted into a movie.

> John Laroche is a tall guy, skinny as a stick, pale-eyed, slouch-shouldered, and sharply handsome, in spite of the fact that he is missing all his front teeth. He has the posture of al dente spaghetti and the nervous intensity of someone who plays a lot of video games.

See what I mean?

Try to identify the sorts of moves the authors make in your example profiles. It's important to read at least several different profiles in order to understand the basic form as well as where you're allowed to try out variations on the theme.

You'll also want to note how the writer handles their own

presence in the profile. In some cases, the profiler becomes a kind of character, a physical presence, rendered through the first person (I). In other cases, the profiler is more of an observer-commenter, obviously present but not seen or heard within the world of the person being profiled.

3. Gather background on your subject.
The first step in a profile is to gather as much readily available background information on your subject as possible. This will be extra important because when you start observing your subject, you will have some context for what you're seeing, and when you interview them, you won't have to ask a bunch of questions you already know the answer to. (Though you may want to confirm any important information that could wind up in the profile.)

4. Observe your subject.
Act like an anthropologist and spend some time watching what your subject does and how they do it in their natural habitat. Take notes on what you're seeing, hearing etc. You should also include your subjective impressions of the subject, since you're trying to create a rounded picture of the whole person. Try to be as unobtrusive as possible. If things occur about which you're curious and have questions, file those away for the interview.

5. Interview your subject.
Once you've had a chance to observe your subject, arrange for a time to sit down for a more formal interview. It need not be long, but you will want to speak to them directly. Make sure to plan ahead of time what you want to ask and arrange to record the exchange (with the subject's permission). The more planning and preparation, the better the interview. Your background research and observations may give you sufficient material for your questions, but if you're feeling stuck,

look at your model profiles for the kinds of questions those writers ask. Or explore any of the approximately ten zillion interview-based podcasts out there for inspiration.

6. *Review your material.*
Before drafting, take some time to go back over all you've gathered. Even for a short profile like you're doing here, you'll find you've gathered a tremendous amount of stuff, and it helps to take a minute and remind yourself of what you have.

7. *Draft the profile.*
As always, remember your audience as you write your initial draft. Hook them at the beginning, and deliver on that promise through the remainder of the profile. If you find yourself getting stuck, go back to the model profiles to see how they work. If you're having trouble with flow, just write a bunch of individual paragraphs you feel are interesting all by themselves. Later you can go back and arrange these bits and link them together.

8. *Test your draft.*
Ask a test reader or two to read the profile and rate it on a scale of one to ten, with one being, "I'd rather jam knitting needles into my own eyes than to have to read this profile again," and ten being, "Nuclear Armageddon could have been exploding all around me and still I couldn't have stopped reading this profile."

After the rating, ask the test reader to give you a sentence or two of feedback explaining their rating.

9. *Revise, edit, polish.*
Based on the feedback from your test audience, as well as your own reflection on your draft, revise the profile to completion.

REFLECT

For me, the most difficult part of this kind of writing is approaching the subject and then doing the interview. By nature I'm a bit shy and don't like to impose myself on people, and while I enjoy learning about others, the interviews can often seem sort of awkward, with the subject feeling self-conscious about being interviewed, and me feeling self-conscious about grilling them.

But over time, I've become much better at overcoming these predispositions. A lot of it is simply repetition—what was once scary has become less so with frequent exposure. I'll always feel some anxiety about this kind of work, but I no longer let that anxiety stop me from doing what I need to do.

In many ways, as I look back and reflect, I seem like a whole different person. As a student, I was always hesitant to raise my hand and share in class, not because I thought I might have a wrong answer, but because I just didn't want the attention, even if I was right.

Now, as a teacher and sometime public speaker, I may be presenting to hundreds of people at a time, their attention on me and my ideas. Even thinking about doing this can bring back a measure of anxiety, but I've done it often enough I know that I will be able to do it again.

And doing things that do not come naturally can feel pretty empowering. I am not a whole different person. I am the same shy kid I've always been. I now know how to take care of that shy kid while not letting him stop me from something I want to do.

This is a roundabout way of asking you reflect on the role anxiety may have played in your writing practice and see if you can identify ways you've developed to address these anxieties.

Who Is This Special Person?

(Tribute)

This experience is related to "Who Is This Stranger?" in obvious ways, in that it is designed to present another human being to the audience, but there's a big difference in that this is a person with whom you are well acquainted.

This seems easy, writing about a person you know whose work and/or life you're intimately familiar with. No problem, right?

But actually this is what makes it so difficult. Often when people are important and familiar to us, we tend to take them for granted, as they are simply part of the foundation on which our life is built. We stop seeing them clearly.

This is a practical experience, as at some point in your life you may need to honor another person by introducing them to an audience.

Presenting an award, a best man's or maid of honor's speech, a birthday or graduation, introducing a speaker, the foreword to a book, a eulogy—all could present occasions to pay tribute to a person who is important to you and to others.

AUDIENCE

You are writing for people who are interested in hearing about why this person is being honored. A tribute is almost always attached to an occasion that triggers the tribute, so the audience expectations will be inextricably tied to that occasion. A tribute at a retirement party is different from a tribute at a funeral.

Let the occasion dictate your audience's needs, attitudes, and knowledge regarding the person you're paying tribute to.

In many cases, the person being paid tribute to will also be present, so keep this in mind.

PROCESS

1. Choose the subject and occasion.
As straightforward as it sounds, choose someone you'd like to honor and then an occasion at which they'll be honored.

2. Analyze the audience.
Knowing the person and occasion will help you determine the needs, attitudes, and knowledge of your audience. It will help you with tone and should even direct you toward appropriate content. You'll also want to think about these audience elements in the context of the questions the audience will bring to the occasion, questions such as the following:

1. Who is this person?

2. Why are they being honored?

3. Seriously, what makes them so special?

3. Brainstorm material.

Think of a tribute as a kind of argument in which you are offering a claim (this person is special and deserves recognition) and supplying supporting evidence and illustrations to support that claim.

Brainstorm material that will prove to be sufficient and compelling evidence for your audience, and don't forget to keep it appropriate to the occasion.

4. Draft.

As you write, be aware of the appropriate length. You aren't the star of the show. You're just the warm-up act.

5. Try out your tribute.

Tributes are best appreciated when read aloud. Find some willing listeners who are not the person being honored and see how they respond. If they can answer the questions from the audience section, you're probably on target. Make sure you've written a tribute, not a roast. A tribute gone wrong can be entertaining to the audience but offensive to the person you're supposed to be honoring.

6. Revise, edit, polish.

Think how great it will feel to have this ready to go if you ever have need.

REFLECT

This will be a little awkward and you never need to show it to anyone, but imagine you were to write a tribute to yourself. What would you want included? What do you hope someone else would say about you if and when the occasion for you to be honored arises?

REMIX

Set your tribute to video and music. Take your tribute and turn it into a multimedia presentation complete with voice-over, visuals, and backing music.

The Right Word vs.
the Almost Right Word

(Thinking about Sentences)

Mark Twain famously said, "The difference between the almost right word and the right word is really a large matter. It's the difference between the lightning bug and the lightning."

Twain meant that small changes in language can create significant shifts in impact, the difference between the soft glow of a lightning bug and the sudden total illumination afforded by the lightning.

To illustrate, two sentences:

I have smelled what suntan lotion smells like spread over 21,000 pounds of hot skin.

And

I have smelled what suntan lotion smells like spread over 21,000 pounds of hot flesh.

To which of these sentences did you have an emotionally visceral response, perhaps a kind of cringe?

Almost certainly the second sentence, which appeared in an essay by David Foster Wallace called "A Supposedly Fun Thing I'll Never Do Again." In the essay, he writes about his experience on a weeklong cruise to the Bahamas. If you couldn't tell by the title or the sentence, the author did not find the experience enjoyable.

The first sentence is my inferior alteration of the original.

Flesh, flesh, flesh, flesh, flesh. Is there a grosser word in the English language? If there is, it would be "moist." Moist . . . flesh.

Shudder.

One of the key skills for writers is to develop a sensitivity to using the right word versus the almost right word.

For this experience, you're going to practice this skill for the benefit of an interested audience.

You will be creating a work of analysis and argument claiming a particular word choice is right and then explaining why you believe this to be true.

AUDIENCE

Your readers are interested in writing and like to spend time thinking about the kinds of language choices writers make and the different impacts of those choices. They want to be turned on to other examples that will help increase their sensitivity to these choices.

PROCESS

1. Find an example sentence.

There are two possible routes.

You can find what seems to be a perfect sentence that you can then alter to make less perfect, like I demonstrated above when I substituted "skin" for "flesh."

Or you can identify a good to very good sentence that you think could be made better by altering a word or two (but not more than that). You're not rewriting an entire sentence; you're looking for examples to illustrate the right word versus the almost right word.

Create your two versions of the sentence: one that clearly has the right word and one that has an acceptable but also inferior alternative.

2. Build your analysis.
Why is one word right and the other almost right? Think of the impact word choice has on the audience in the context of the sentence, first in isolation and then in terms of the larger piece of writing the sentence comes from.

What is lost with the almost right word versus the right word?

3. Draft.
Now, considering your audience, draft your argument and analysis. You want to be careful to give them sufficient context about the text your sentence comes from so they can properly appreciate the argument and analysis to come.

4. Revise, edit, polish.
Each step of the way you should gain a little additional insight into your sentence, your appreciation for its "rightness" growing the more you consider it. I first read the sentence from "A Supposedly Fun Thing I'll Never do Again" more than twenty years ago, and it took me fifteen years, including having assigned the essay in classes several times, before I fully recognized the genius of his use of "smells" and "smells like." The repetition of "smells" actually causes the reader to smell twice, conjuring that specific suntan lotion scent in a more powerful way than a more syntactically straightforward version like "I have smelled suntan lotion spread over 21,000 pounds of hot flesh."

REFLECT

How much time do you spend on your writing to find the right words? Or maybe a better question is, how much time do you have when you're writing to be able to pursue the right word or even the almost right word as opposed to the probably good enough word?

A tough part about most writing is how it must be done in tight time windows that may not leave sufficient time for an idea to gel, and if the idea doesn't gel, it's difficult to start worrying about polishing a piece to the highest possible shine.

One way to gain additional time for revision, editing, and polishing is to try to start the drafting process earlier, to have more time later. (I know, easier said than done.)

This is a good opportunity to reflect on your writing process in this context and see if there are steps you can take to make more space for the parts of the process for which there never seem to be enough time.

THIS IS THE END

Remember the quote from Jeff O'Neal: "You are going to spend your whole life learning to write, and then you are going to die"?

If you've completed a good number of these experiences, you've had a chance to develop your writing practice. As our practices evolve, it's easy to lose sight of how far we've come. In graduate school, I had to produce a book-length thesis. In my case, it was a collection of short stories. I'd worked on the stories for three years with monklike devotion, and by the end of my studies—at age twenty-seven—I figured I was pretty far along on my journey as a writer.

Now, I'd never actually published a short story, but I thought that was just a matter of time, of putting a story in front of the right editor at the right time, of getting lucky. I did publish a story (the one discussed in the chapter on titles) about a year after graduation, and then another, and another, and then lots of other different kinds of writing, and so on and so on, until twenty years later, when I've reached the point where this will be my seventh book.

Looking back at it that way, I'm astonished by my own life: that I've grown so old, but also that I've made a career of the kind of work I spent hours and hours dedicating myself to during graduate school.

A year or so ago, I pulled my graduate thesis off the shelf where it lives in my living room. I don't know if it's still the case, but at the time one bound copy of every thesis went into the university library, and one went to the graduating student. I hadn't looked at the stories in many years. Some of them I hadn't thought about since my graduation.

I was surprised by what I found, but I shouldn't have been. It's not that the stories were bad, exactly, but neither were they good. With hindsight, I recognized the writer who was crafting those stories was not yet ready to be published. There is a clear difference between the stories in my thesis and those that would be published.

When I look at my first published stories versus the fiction I write now, I can see significant additional growth. I've been writing professionally for not quite twenty years, and yet I know that, in many ways, I'm just getting started. There's much better work in my future than my past.

The same is true for everyone, so this isn't the *end* end; it's just the end of one part of a much longer journey.

Taking a moment to reflect on where you've come from and where you're going seems appropriate.

Who Are You Now?
(As a Writer)

(This Is the End . . .

of This Book)

Now that you've been through some writing experiences, are you a different writer?

What kind of writer are you now?

When do you write? How do you write? What are your attitudes toward writing?

AUDIENCE

You're writing for the same audience as in the original "Who Are You Now?" experience. They remember your past, but they'd like to hear about your present.

They're curious about how you view your writing abilities and attitudes now that you've had these experiences. They also want you to be fully honest about your experiences, even if they haven't been positive.

PROCESS

1. Consider your writing experiences since you were last asked who you are.

Have your attitudes toward writing changed at all or have they basically stayed the same?

What about how you approach writing? Have you altered your writing process at all?

What do you feel like you can do now that you couldn't do before? What do you know about writing that you didn't know before?

What do you still hope to develop further? Where do you see yourself going with your writing?

2. Draft.

Similar to the original, you're telling a story to help your audience understand how you perceive the journey you've been taking. Think about telling and showing.

3. Revise.

Do your best to make sure your piece says what you intend to say. You want to be honest with your audience while also being appropriately sensitive. You've shared experiences, but they only know their half of the equation.

What do you need to tell your audience in order to fill them in about what has been going on with you?

4. Edit and polish.

The audience will likely be comparing the degree of care and consideration brought to this manuscript with the original attempt. What changes can you demonstrate?

REFLECT

Same questions as the first time:

How diverse are your writing experiences? Have you done lots of different things, or do you feel like you've mostly done variations of the same thing?

Which sounds more true to you: "I am a good/bad writer," or "I am good/bad at writing"?

How much (if any) of your attitudes about writing are linked to what happened in school and/or grades?

When have you most enjoyed writing? When have you least enjoyed it? What is the difference between those experiences?

REMIX

Choose any of the experiences you completed and revise the parameter or process to make it more useful to those engaging with the experience.

Make sure to support and explain your choices so the originator of the experience understands why you're recommending these changes.

Appendix

Possible Routes through This Book

While I hope that many people will read and use this book outside of a class context, for those who are interested in using it in a class context, I've mapped out some possible routes through the book that may apply to specific courses with specific objectives.

These are just blueprints, open to adjustment and interpretation, reflective of how I've used these assignments in my own career. If I've learned one thing from teaching, it's that the plan is only the beginning, and the best courses rise from paying specific attention to the needs of the students one is working with. Necessary adjustments are highly encouraged.

TRADITIONAL FIRST-YEAR WRITING

This route follows a path (or paths) that I would use myself in a first-year writing course (what used to be called "freshman composition") with a traditional or academic focus. It's designed to give students experience with the full range of the writer's practice while also making sure to introduce them to specific skills of research and source citation, which may be expected as part of the curriculum.

WEEK 1	**Before We Begin** Who Are You? (As a Writer)
WEEKS 2–4	**The Writer's Practice** How Do I . . . ? (Instructions) Should I . . . ? (Review)
WEEK 5	**Skills Drills** Who Are They? (Profiling)
WEEKS 6–7	**Analytical Experiences** *Choose One:* Who Are We? (Rhetorical Analysis of a Commercial) or What's So Funny? (Rhetorical Analysis of a Work of Humor)
WEEKS 8–9	**Argument Experiences** What Do They Mean? (Argument Summary and Response) Why Should I Trust This? (Understanding Sources)
WEEKS 10–11	**Argument Experiences cont.** Argument as Conversation *Choose One:* Is a Hot Dog a Sandwich? (Impossible Argument) or You've Got to Do This (Passion Argument)
WEEKS 11–15	**Argument Experiences cont.** Why Am I So Angry? (Problem/Solution Argument)
WEEK 16	**Reflection** Who Are You Now? (As a Writer) (This Is the End . . . of This Book)

ALTERNATIVE FIRST-YEAR WRITING

Over my years of teaching first-year writing, I've grown more and more frustrated with an experience bound by a "research paper." I'm convinced asking students to go from zero to a fully formed and well-researched topic that is then turned into a finished argument in the span of four to five weeks (which may be a generous amount of time) is a nearly impossible task. I'll put it this way: I would not have thrived on some of my own past assignments. I've found the "Why Am I So Angry?" (Problem/Solution Argument) approach a good way to include researched argument without running afoul of too many difficulties, but I also am a proponent of first-year writing curricula that stop short of requiring students to write that final argument. By eliminating the final paper, I've found that the depth of *thinking* and research students do on their topics can be much improved, since they're spending less time and energy fretting about turning in the big final project.

If you're an instructor looking for a different way of engaging in the kinds of thinking students must practice to be good academic researchers, this route may be of interest.

WEEK 1	Before We Begin Who Are You? (As a Writer)
WEEKS 2–4	The Writer's Practice How Do I ...? (Instructions) Should I ...? (Review)
WEEK 5–7	Skills Drills Who Are They? (Profiling) If It Isn't True, Why Do People Believe It?
WEEKS 8–10	Analytical Experiences *Choose One:* Who Are We? (Rhetorical Analysis of a Commercial) or What's So Funny? (Rhetorical Analysis of a Work of Humor) *Choose One:* What's Going to Happen? (Playing the Pundit) or What If ...? (Alternate History) or How's It All Going to End? (Judging the Apocalypse)
WEEKS 11–12	Argument Experiences Why Should I Trust This? (Understanding Sources)
WEEK 13	Argument Experiences cont. Is a Hot Dog a Sandwich? (Impossible Argument) You've Got to Do This (Passion Argument)
WEEKS 14–15	Argument Experiences cont. Hey, Whaddaya Know? (Trivia Questions and Annotated Bibliography) May I ...? (Proposal)
WEEK 16	Reflection Who Are You Now? (As a Writer) (This Is the End ... of This Book)

REALLY ALTERNATIVE FIRST-YEAR WRITING

If I had total freedom, unencumbered by curricular guidelines or other external forces, this is the sequence I would use for a first-year writing course. This results in students writing more total words as well as tackling a greater variety of assignments.

In this kind of sequence, the grading/assessment is more focused on the production and process and reflection portions of the experiences than on judging the assignments using traditional grading. The goal is to get students writing as much as possible and to build on their base of knowledge and experience from one assignment to another.

WEEK 1	Before We Begin Who Are You? (As a Writer)
WEEK 2	The Writer's Practice Should I ...? (Review)
WEEKS 3-5	Skills Drills Who Are They? (Profiling) Where Did You Go? (Sense Memory) You Did What? (Adventure Report) Is It True? Did It Really Happen? (Experience vs. Memory)
WEEK 6	Having Some Fun Make Me Laugh (Jokes) or No, Seriously, Make Me Laugh (Short Imagined Monologue)
WEEKS 7-8	Understanding the World Why Should I Trust This? (Understanding Sources) What's Going to Happen? (Playing the Pundit) or What If ...? (Alternate History) or How's It All Going to End? (Judging the Apocalypse)
WEEKS 9-11	Argument Fun Are You Trying to Make Me Angry? (Conflict Letter) How Can I Help You Help Me? (Solution Letter) *Choose One:* Is a Hot Dog a Sandwich? (Impossible Argument) or You've Got to Do This! (Passion Argument)
WEEK 11	Circling Back The Right Word v. the Almost Right Word (Thinking about Sentences)
WEEKS 12-15	Reflection Who Is This Special Person? (Tribute) What Should I Do? (Advice to Someone Else) Who Are You Now? (As a Writer) (This Is the End ... of This Book)

Acknowledgments

There are simply too many people to list when it comes to acknowledging those who have influenced my teaching, a list that would include every one of the thousands of students with whom I've shared a classroom, as well as the teachers and colleagues who have influenced my approach. Education is a collaborative enterprise, and this book wouldn't exist without all of the people with whom I've crossed paths over the years.

While all of the experiences in this book are stamped with my imprint, a number of them have specific roots with others, and I want to acknowledge them here. At the same time, I want to encourage others to feel free to take these experiences and remake and recombine them in any way they see fit.

The instructions for making a peanut butter and jelly sandwich originates from my third grade teacher, Mrs. Goldman, who was the first to introduce me to writing experiences and the rhetorical situation.

"Where Did You Go? (Sense Memory) was inspired by my graduate school professor at McNeese St. University, Robert Olen Butler, whose book *From Where You Dream: The Process of Writing Fiction* offers much more insight into the role sense memory plays in writing.

"You Did What?" (Adventure Report) originated with my college professor at the University of Illinois, Philip Graham.

"Are You Trying to Make Me Angry?" (Conflict Letter) and "How Can I Help You Help Me?" (Solution Letter) originated with Dr. Marlene Preston, my faculty supervisor at Virginia Tech.